"I've worked and met countless people throughout my career, but Korena is one of the few that continually inspires me. Her passion for life, for her family, and for her team is like none other. She has a contagious drive to make life better for others and has overcome countless obstacles with a strength rarely seen. Korena as a person has created a strong brand, which contributes to the strong brand created for her company, KeyMedia."

**—SHARON KNOLL**, VP, Client Services, Media One

"Korena is an extraordinarily successful business owner who hasn't forgotten what it means to be an authentic human being. She devotes her time not only to her family, her clients, and her team but to her community as well. As a mom and a business owner myself, I'm always inspired by her example."

**—SUSAN BAIER**, Founder and President, Audience Audit

"I met Korena when she was a media planner at a regional advertising agency in Sioux Falls. As we worked together over the years (me as a vendor to her), we became good friends. I remember when she went to a small digital startup and found out within the first few days that the partners in the firm decided to quit but gave their seat on the digital programmatic exchange desk to Korena. I was a little concerned for her, but I also knew that she was smart and determined. And that programmatic digital had huge promise—this was early on for that aspect of the advertising world. Sure enough, within a few years, Korena was running a mid-size digital agency, picking up regional and national business and employing a dozen smart young people. I was very impressed when I heard the story about why her mantra is to balance business with personal life. She has proven that you can run a successful, thriving company with that philosophy, which is exciting to see. Korena has shown that you can work your way from a very difficult situation to a thriving business and family life. She's an inspiration to everyone!"

**—TOM SMULL**, President, Associations Inc.

"Korena Keys is not just a business leader and marketing expert; she is a community advocate. Her local pride and her commitment to showcasing the best of South Dakota are truly inspiring. Her events are not just gatherings but celebrations of the community, bringing together individuals who share her passion and love for the region.

Korena is an exceptional business leader who embodies the spirit of community engagement and promotion. Her dedication to South Dakota and her ability to bring people together to celebrate its unique qualities make her an invaluable asset to her community. I wholeheartedly recommend Korena Keys for her outstanding contributions and her unwavering commitment to promoting and uplifting the local community."

**—DOUGLAS KARR**, Digital Transformation Author,
Speaker, Consultant

"When I first met Korena, all I saw was a successful, smart business owner. But as I've gotten to know her over the years, I've learned about her life's challenges and watched how she has taken every life lesson and put it to good use to become the remarkable human being she is today.

Her integrity and resilience are second to none. Her commitment to creating life-changing opportunities for her employees is deeply held and her love for her family goes down to her core.

Korena's story is one of tenacity, faith, and the good things that come to good people who refuse to give in or give up. Prepare to be more grateful for what you have, more committed to be better, and more inspired to make a difference in any way that you can."

**—DREW MCLELLAN**, CEO, Partner,
Agency Management Institute

# FROM
# WELFARE
## TO
# CEO

KORENA KEYS

# FROM
# WELFARE
## TO
# CEO

LESSONS FROM A
**SINGLE MOM'S JOURNEY**
IN **ENTREPRENEURSHIP**

*Advantage* | Books

Published by Advantage Books, Charleston, South Carolina.
An imprint of Advantage Media.

ADVANTAGE is a registered trademark, and the Advantage colophon is a trademark of Advantage Media Group, Inc.

Printed in the United States of America.

10  9  8  7  6  5  4  3  2  1

ISBN: 978-1-64225-594-2 (Paperback)
ISBN: 978-1-64225-593-5 (eBook)

Library of Congress Control Number: 2023922819

Cover design by Analisa Smith.
Layout design by Lance Buckley.

This publication is designed to provide accurate and authoritative information in regard to the subject matter covered. It is sold with the understanding that the publisher is not engaged in rendering legal, accounting, or other professional services. If legal advice or other expert assistance is required, the services of a competent professional person should be sought.

Advantage Books is an imprint of Advantage Media Group. Advantage Media helps busy entrepreneurs, CEOs, and leaders write and publish a book to grow their business and become the authority in their field. Advantage authors comprise an exclusive community of industry professionals, idea-makers, and thought leaders. For more information go to **advantagemedia.com**.

*For my children and grandchildren, that they may know how they changed my life for the better. My prayer for them is to avoid the heartbreaks and struggles and learn from my mistakes.*

# Contents

# Acknowledgments

I would not be here today if it was not for the love, support, and guidance received along the way.

Mom and Dad, you taught me perseverance and compassion.

Kamie, Cole, and Kaylee—because of you I learned patience and love, and you gave me the *why* behind my drive.

To Marsha, my friend and confidant, thank you for all the early morning walks, late-night glasses of wine, and encouragement to keep going.

To the coaches and mentors along the way—Jo Garner, Paul Ten Haken, Chris Kinney, Nancy Roberts, Wade Humphreys, Pat Azzera, Tom Morgan, Drew McLellan, and Kurt Whitesel—thank you for believing in me and sharing your wisdom.

For every employee who showed up and helped shape KeyMedia Solutions, thank you!

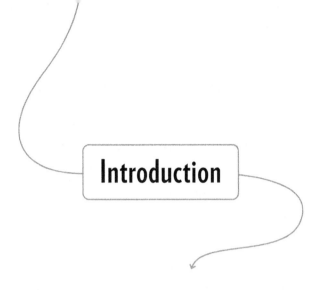

# Introduction

**H**ave you ever been told not to aspire to something higher? We have that in common. I've been told I can't have my dreams come true and that I should settle for something less. It would have been easy to nod my head and go along with other people's low expectations for me, but I couldn't settle for that. Whenever someone doubted me and my capabilities, I would train my mind's eye on a goal above and beyond my present circumstance and tell myself I'd get there. It might not be today, but I would.

I did get there. I met my goals, over and over again, and now I'm the CEO of my own award-winning, nationally recognized digital marketing company. My success didn't happen overnight, and there were stumbles along the way, but I'm happy, prosperous, and optimistic that nothing can stop me. I wake up each day ready to work hard at a job I love in a career that brings me joy. I'm devoted to my family, faith, friends, colleagues, and my community and advocate for them wherever and whenever the opportunity presents itself.

In other words, I'm living my life to the fullest, and it's a great feeling. I want that for you, too. My ultimate personal satisfaction is in helping others feel the glow that comes with a hard-earned win. I love to coach, mentor, and witness people around me learn and grow.

## Feeling Trapped Doesn't Have to Hold You Back

Just know that the challenges you've faced in life don't have to hold you back from success. I don't say that lightly, either. I know sometimes it feels as though we're trapped by our problems. It's happened to me many times, both with acute emergencies and with chronic hassles that I just couldn't shake. It's a very difficult place to be in mentally and emotionally. How can you escape a situation when it saps you of the energy you need to find your way out of it? It's very easy to spiral down into confusion and frustration.

When I found out I was pregnant as a junior in high school, I was stuck between a rock and a hard place with two tough choices: bringing up my baby when I wasn't prepared to be a mother or giving her away for adoption. Either way, I knew I was in for a great deal of sacrifice and emotional turmoil.

We can feel trapped in a million ways. Maybe it's the tattoo on your shoulder or the color of your hair or your skin color, gender, sexual orientation, or religion that comes with assumptions on the part of others who don't want to see the individual you are. They confine you to a box of preconceived notions in their heads, and sometimes those notions are outright prejudices that can hold you back from opportunities to achieve your potential. For me, it was being a teen mom.

If you see hurdles complicating your path forward, it's only natural to worry about whether you'll ever meet your goals. I'm here to tell you that you can and should hold on to your dreams and pursue them, *no matter the obstacles in your way.*

I was seventeen, and my daughter's bio-dad didn't want anything to do with her or me. I was in school, and my parents were not in a position to financially support us. I struggled for years from paycheck to paycheck, and sometimes I didn't have enough money to cover my bills.

I'd almost lost my business and had to fight extremely hard to keep it afloat, working night and day to come up with workable solutions. I've had personal setbacks, too, like my divorce that threatened my sense of self-worth.

But I made it through. It wasn't easy. I did it with sheer grit and a lot of faith. It was scary and confusing sometimes, and many times I felt like every door was closed to me. But instead of surrendering to that fear, I persisted. I survived. Even better, I thrived. My trials made me grow. I couldn't see it at the time, but they were the stepping stones to my success now. I was determined to be better, and even at the lowest of my lows, I never forgot that.

You're meant for something better, too.

You might say it's easy for me to use such optimistic language. I don't know your problems. Talking about grit and faith might sound like a cliché to you. That's what everyone says, right? How can you have grit when every door gets slammed in your face? Isn't faith for people who have options?

I feel you, and my heart goes out to you. Of course, I can't know your exact struggles or circumstances. But I genuinely care. And I hope that by reading my story, you'll see that your own unique set of circumstances doesn't define the road you'll travel. *You create the map.* You're stronger than all the conditions that come together to shape your life.

I promise you that those tried-and-true pep talks we've heard over and over are there for a reason—they work. You can find a way to make them work for you, too. If you're still not convinced, look at it this way: Aren't you tired of negative people throwing cold water on your plans? Or dissing your passion, whatever that passion is?

Whatever we do, we don't want those people to get the last word. No way. A little stubborn perseverance can go a long way! And maybe your good example will equip other people with the courage to step into their story. And with that courage comes empowerment. I want my grandchildren to feel they can do anything and be anything they dream of being. I want that for all our children.

Coming from the viewpoint of a woman in a male-dominated industry, I also have a special place in my heart for encouraging other women to follow their dreams. In this book I'd like to speak with particular concern to the challenges of women in the workplace. Very often we serve as caregivers in both our homes and in our offices. I look forward to sharing my personal philosophy that balance isn't always feasible, and so rather than focusing all my energies on that daunting task, I reframed my thinking. I now try to blend, not balance. It's a distinction I'll go into, and I hope it will be of some help to you.

## What I'll Cover in This Book

I love details and going deep into real conversation, so my book will span a lot of territory. I'm hoping the wide-ranging subject matter, from personal to professional to spiritual, will help spark discussions among you, my readers, and inspire you to look inside yourselves to find the strength, creativity, and commitment to being your best selves. I've added guides throughout each chapter to remind you of my main points, including (1) sidebars with important questions to consider as you read; (2) Thoughtshots, ideas meant to spark conversation; and (3) a tip of the hat to my home state of South Dakota with my "You Betcha" words of wisdom at the end of each chapter that I've accrued over the years.

I'll start with my childhood and how it set me up to navigate challenging situations. I learned at a very young age that change is hard. It's really, *really* hard! And it never stops, as the rest of my story will prove. But hand in hand with change comes growth. That's where you'll reap your rewards. By the time you turn the last page, I hope you'll feel inspired to step out of your comfort zone and strive to reach your greatest potential. Let's look up and see what could be—by choosing to believe in ourselves.

# Where My Story Begins

*I love to see a young girl go out
and grab the world by the lapels.*
**—MAYA ANGELOU**

Look up. Seriously, please join me, and look up from this page right now. I'll wait!

Whatever you see, whether you're staring at a fluorescent light, a spider web in the corner of the room, the moon, or an airplane leaving contrails across the sky, looking up gets you away—for a valuable second—from what you're doing in the current moment.

In a way, looking up wakes us up. A lot of us stay on autopilot at work and home for most of our lives. We're content not to rock the boat. We're OK with being only sort of happy, if not all of the time, then most of the time. We tend to ignore that inner voice that says we aren't living up to our potential. Doing all right is just fine, we tell ourselves. And, of course, plenty of us can't even manage being somewhat happy. We're depressed. Confused about next steps. Or just plain exhausted.

Wherever you are right now—a good place, a bad one, or somewhere in the middle—just know that no matter how you feel, when you look up from your life, what you see doesn't matter half as much as what you've accomplished by raising your gaze: *you've changed your perspective.* It might be a new view, or one you've looked upon before and either forgot about or simply grown accustomed to. But you're snapped out of your complacency and reminded that every moment counts and every action you take matters.

It's such a simple thing, looking up, and not something that automatically comes to mind to do. Nowadays, we tend to alternate between getting distracted and hyper-focusing, don't we? Take a look around you right now, and see who's locked onto a screen! Almost everyone, right? But by taking a symbolic first step of tilting our chins up and raising our eyes heavenward, we're validating our dreams. We're moving toward becoming the people we are truly meant to be.

I told you I'd be looking up with you. Guess where I am right now? I'm at an Airbnb with the people I love, at a desk beneath a window of a little office, looking up at the Sandias, a gorgeous chain of mountains near Albuquerque, New Mexico. They're breathtaking. Whether I'm on vacation or at home, I get up between five and six every morning to work out and have some alone time. Right now, I'm watching the morning sun come up over a mountain crest. It's humbling and gorgeous and just so beautiful. To be able to sit here and experience it is pretty awe-inspiring.

You might wonder how finding genuine fulfillment can be as simple as indulging in a change of scenery. Just because I reframe my view doesn't mean the problems I encounter go away. Nope. They're still there. It's a well-known fact of life that a lot of what happens is out of our control, but when we choose to change our gaze, we're acknowledging that we're at least partially responsible for our destiny. We're claiming our space. We're playing those cards we've been dealt. We're doing our part. When we look up, we're showing gratitude for the life we've been given: we can thank our Higher Power, be open to possibilities, consider our goals, and step outside ourselves, too.

Here in Albuquerque I can't help but marvel at how magnificent that sun and these mountains are and how small I am in comparison. I call it going on a Nature Date. Every moment I spend communing with nature, I feel like I've become a calmer, wiser, happier person. I highly recommend you go on a Nature Date at least once a week. Recognizing my smallness doesn't make me feel bad—quite the opposite! Nature at its most glorious makes me feel that any problems in my life are manageable. After all, I'm taking up only a little space on the miraculous tapestry that is our world, our universe. Immersing myself in natural beauty puts all my worries in perspective. Time marches on, yet the Sandia Mountains are still standing, changing ever so slowly, unfazed by our daily business.

I have an additional reason to celebrate being here and looking up at these craggy mountains and that vivid pink sunrise. This trip I'm taking with my family is part of a dream come true—a dream I've worked toward for many years, and now it's real. More than anything, I have wanted to travel the world with the people I love. This trip is only one of many we've taken together.

I didn't grow up with a lot of money. I didn't travel a lot. We took a couple of family vacations, but most of them we went to stay with extended family, like my grandparents or an aunt and uncle. And that's OK—I am grateful for those opportunities to play with my cousins. But I didn't get to experience a lot of this world. So when I finally was able to travel a little for work, I was bitten by the travel bug. It hit me that there's this great wide world out there that's amazing, and if at all possible, we need to experience it. Travel broadens our minds and our perspectives, and it gives us insights into other people's lives that we don't have when we don't get to travel or we're not willing to go and try new things. I was in my thirties before I set my first bucket list goal of visiting, and staying overnight, in each of the fifty states before my fiftieth birthday.

When I travel, I act a bit like a tourist because there are certain places and events I want to scratch off my bucket list. But I mainly focus on doing what the locals do. I want to know what life looks like for them: what they eat, where they hang out if they have a day off from work, or what an ordinary day in their culture is like. I want authenticity.

Nothing brings me greater joy than seeing my young grand-daughters, Ivy and Iris, along with my grandson, Adler, widen their eyes at the incredible vistas they see on our trips together. It warms my heart. It makes me feel good. And now I've got grandbaby Kyra to enjoy watching when she gets big enough to appreciate our vacations!

From the time my grandchildren were small, my Christmas present to them has been an experience, not a toy. The older ones have gotten used to that, and they start saying right after Christmas, "I can't wait to go to _____!" They'll talk about getting ready for it, and after we all come back, they'll chatter about our adventures for six months.

They're getting to be so brave. Last year we were in Florida, and all Ivy wanted to do was see an alligator and eat an alligator! Which she did. My grandkids have been to more places and been able to experience more things than I had when I was thirty, and that fills my heart with joy. I'm thrilled to see their passion and their excitement to go out and experience new adventures. Now they have stories to share. It's a beautiful thing. We're creating wonderful family memories together.

But there's a bigger benefit: through our travels, they're also creating their own identities. The trips help shape their view of the world, how they fit into it, and how other people do, too.

I want them to look up, always, and wonder at this beautiful planet we inhabit. I want them to look up and realize that the way they most often see things isn't necessarily the only way, or even the best way, and that other people often see things differently. When the day comes that my grandchildren are able to step outside themselves like that on their own, without prodding from their parents or grandparents, I will rest easy about their futures because anyone who understands that they have options—apart from what they see right in front of their faces—will be able to survive any problem and thrive under any conditions.

That's what I want for the people I love. And that's what I want for *you*! I especially hope that you'll be able to realize your greatest dreams. It's an amazing feeling that I have achieved mine. Bringing happiness to my family, helping one another learn how to live against the backdrop of a world teeming with both opportunity and obstacles, light and darkness, joy and suffering, is such a fulfilling thing to do.

Ultimately, my dream is about bringing to my kids and grandkids a sense that they can do this on their own—without me. Because let's face it, someday these family vacations will end. Someday, we will pass from this earth. I have no doubt I'll go long before the Sandia Mountain range crumbles into dust. And I'm OK with that as long as I know I did my best, strove to reach my potential, and inspired my loved ones, members of my community, and even perfect strangers to do the same.

Looking up can mean taking stock of where you are and where you've been. Where we've been doesn't define where we can go. That's up to us. But acknowledging our past and being grateful for lessons we learned there can help us move forward.

Whatever your childhood was like, just know that you can start saying yes to new things when you're scared. You will get through the fear and do it anyway, and if you screw up, you don't beat yourself up. You find the silver lining, or any lesson you can, and you keep moving forward.

I'm a case in point—I was a shy kid in a big Catholic family filled with fearless types who valued their independence—typical American farmers with a proud heritage of surviving come hell or high water. You'd never have looked at me and thought, "That little girl hiding in the corner is going to grow up to create a very successful company, mentor people, and become a leader in her community." Hah! No way.

But somehow I did, and it's really not a mystery. Over and over, I was given messages that encouraged me to take risks and be OK with failure. I don't think my parents were actively trying to mold me that way; it was just part of who we were, and it rubbed off on me.

My point is, you can be *taught* to be brave and to take risks. It never came naturally to me. Ever. But by being brought up in a modest household where I felt safe and secure, I was able to step out, little by little, into exploring the world and spinning optimistic dreams for my future.

My parents were blue-collar people, raised in rural South Dakota by hardworking families. They went to tech schools and were smart and resourceful, but where I came from, going to a four-year college wasn't the expectation. There was plenty of work to be had if you were willing and open to learning. My father, Ken, was an electrician. We moved a lot for his work. We lived in Austin, Texas, for about two years, and in Minnesota for a little over a year, and we spent a summer in Missouri to visit Dad when he had to work there for a while. Otherwise, most of my childhood was spent in South Dakota. It's the heartland, a wholesome area of the country that leans on familiar traditions. Not exactly a place you imagine as an incubator churning out risk-taking entrepreneurs, especially female ones!

My mother, Vicky, shone as a traditional homemaker. She had four children in six years and chose to stay at home with us while we were little. I'm wedged between my two brothers: Jim is fifteen months older than I am, and Chris is thirteen months younger. I also have a sister, Bobbi, who is four years younger. Once Bobbi started school, Mom went to work in food services for the local school district to maintain a similar schedule as us four.

As a child, I was blissfully unaware of my parents' financial struggles. I mean, I knew we were not rich, but I didn't feel like we were poor, either. We always had the necessities. We ate well, and Mom made a lot of our clothes when we were young. I remember that the first time we actually went to the store to buy outfits for school was a really big deal.

I vividly recall my mother vacuuming and sweeping the floors every single day, probably because she had to with all of us running around. But I look back now and think, oh my gosh, I never would've done that! She kept the household running so smoothly. Every Saturday she baked multiple loaves of bread from scratch, so there was bread for my dad's lunches and meals for the week.

The whole neighborhood knew that Saturday routine! The first loaves would come out of the oven somewhere around two o'clock. All of the neighborhood kids would hang around in the yard and wait for my mom to pop open the oven. That first loaf would appear, smelling like heaven, and everybody would run into the house. Mom would slice it up, and we'd have hot bread with butter and homemade rhubarb jam. It was such a treat, and the whole neighborhood looked forward to it.

To cap off the event, we'd have Mom's homemade caramel rolls on Sunday morning. They were the best things in the world. I still haven't found anything that can replace my mother's loaves of bread and her gooey caramel rolls. Is it any wonder I love carbs?

Another way I was provided for and didn't realize was extraordinary—because it was so ordinary for our community to lend a hand to one another—was when my neighbor made bicycles for anyone who needed one. Bill, our friend across the alley, was the area garbage man, so he would collect bike parts that people threw away. Next to his garage, he had stacks of tires and random bike parts. Whenever a child or even an adult needed one, he'd go out to his driveway and assemble a special bicycle just for that person. Every kid within six blocks received their very first bike (and probably the next three) from Bill.

That was our life, and nobody knew any different. We helped one another and made do with what we had. We didn't feel we were missing anything. Our lives were rich with family, neighbors, and friends. We weren't aware that having very little was a disadvantage by many people's standards. As a consequence, material things don't matter to me. What matters is experiences and memories with people I care about.

I was shy, but like my mom and my neighbor who made the bikes, I also tried to nurture other people, sometimes too much! My younger brother, Chris, had to go to speech therapy because he wasn't talking. In fact, he didn't learn how to talk until he was four because he never had to—I did everything for him. I told my mother when Chris was hungry or needed anything. Once I started school and was not there all day, Chris flourished. It was a good lesson for me. Everyone needs to ask for what they want. Handing it to them on a silver platter doesn't do them any favors.

But apart from TV-sit-com-worthy scenarios like my accidentally interfering with Chris's speech development, in general, my days as a child were filled with ordinary moments and a lot of routine. I remember at more than one house we lived in, every day we'd hear the town whistle go off at six o'clock in the evening. Man, you'd better be home at six o'clock for dinner! The food was on the table, and we all ate together. Then as a family, we cleaned up after the meal.

Family was what bound us together. When we did go somewhere, we'd go to my aunt and uncle's house and hang out on the farm with them. Our priority was always being around one another. We kids didn't realize it, but that support is what would sustain us when we left the nest.

My mom and dad were devout churchgoers, a practice that also set me up with a strong foundation of faith. We went every Sunday and sat in the same pew. We were often at church on Wednesday nights, too. Outside of misbehaving in church, there was not a lot we could do to get in trouble apart from disrespecting my mother. If we crossed that line, all Mom had to say was, "Wait until your father gets home!" He was the one we had a healthy fear of, but he never raised his voice or used physical force to discipline us.

I realize now how blessed I was that my parents were big on upholding old-fashioned values. Among them was the idea that God would always look after us, so we had no reason not to be brave. My parents had confidence that as long as we kept our priorities straight—God and family first—we would be OK. With that family philosophy firmly in place, they always encouraged the four of us to try new things. They often made remarks like, "Oh, you haven't done this before. Try it." Or, "What do you have to lose?" And when things didn't go the way we wanted, it wasn't a big deal. They never said, "Well, you shouldn't have done that." Instead, they'd ask, "Well, what did you learn from it? Are you going to try it again? Or will you move on to something else?"

That kind of practical encouragement was all I knew growing up. During summers, holidays, and weekends, we were often kicked out the door after breakfast and chores and didn't come back until the six o'clock whistle. We were told to go play, explore, run around the neighborhood, find our friends, and be busy. We weren't really allowed to sit around in the house. We weren't permitted to watch much television, maybe Saturday morning cartoons and the Sunday night Disney movie. We were also assigned extra chores if we were inside, so we had extra incentive to stay outdoors.

My life was predictable and secure. Because it was, I was able to use my imagination and develop problem-solving skills, which later in life served me well.

One of the best strategies for reminding yourself that there are plenty of other people who have walked hard walks yet succeeded, despite their challenges, is to develop your own Role Model Roster. This is an ever-growing list of the successful people within your circle and in the larger world whom you are inspired by. Of course, they can come from different eras, too. I keep track of why I am moved by the stories of these brave, good people—I'll write out my thoughts about what makes them special—and often I'll include one of their more memorable quotes. You never know when you might need to give a speech, or share a bit of wisdom with a friend, or simply remind yourself of sage words from one of your role models. Often, when I'm overwhelmed, I recall the examples of my favorite role models. In fact, I've also got several Role Model Rosters. In the text box, you'll see one I made specifically about female role models not in my family.

## Role Model Roster

### 1. Jo Garner

Jo was my manager very early in my career but really more of a mentor and coach. Jo taught me everything she knew about media planning, strategy, and the art of negotiations. Often, I would hear her say someone needed an "audio educational experience" (teach them the ways) or "gottsa pound 'em" (when she negotiated deals for her clients). She is also the one who taught me to always ask for what I wanted or needed. The answer may be "no," but it may also be a "yes" or an "I can't do that, but what about this?" If I don't ask, the answer will always be a no.

2. **Jolene Loetscher** *(https://www.facebook.com/hellojolene)*

Jolene is a colleague and friend who took a really traumatic personal experience and used her voice to change South Dakota legislation (Jolene's Law). She then ran for mayor of Sioux Falls (she was close but not successful). She owns multiple successful businesses in Sioux Falls and Omaha, Nebraska. I love that Jolene is focused and determined to take her experiences and improve the lives of others. She is a brilliant businesswoman, political activist, and mom to the cutest little girl.

3. **Sandra Yancey** *(https://sandrayancey.com)*

Sandra saw a need for women business owners to connect and build one another up, so she founded eWomen Network in 2012–2013. I was a member for a few years but with no local chapter was difficult to maintain. The network is now international in reach with 500,000-plus members and 118 chapters and has a foundation that has awarded more than 282 cash grants. Always steadfast in her faith, Sandra's personal mission is "I am an ordinary woman who lives an extraordinary life. I can help you have one too."

4. **Eleanor Roosevelt**

I loved Eleanor Roosevelt's passion for human rights long before it was popular. One of my favorite quotes of hers is "Courage is more exhilarating than fear and in the long run it is easier. We do not have to become heroes overnight. Just one step at a time, meeting each thing that comes up, seeing it is not as dreadful as it appeared, discovering we have the strength to stare it down."

## 5. Princess Diana

Yes, Princess Diana was a strong humanitarian and advocated for AIDS awareness, but she was also an "I don't go by the rule book ... I lead from the heart, not the head" type of person. She had to take on the entire British monarchy, the paparazzi, and the public. And she did it with elegance and grace. Though she appeared soft-spoken and meek, she was a fighter and is famous for having said, "Everyone needs to be valued. Everyone has the potential to give something back."

## 6. Rosa Parks

One of the bravest women in our history, Rosa Parks risked her own life to make a stand and help others. I love her quote, "You must never be fearful about what you are doing when it is right."

I do greatly admire the women I listed on my sample Role Model Roster, but by far my biggest inspiration comes from my own family. Both my sets of grandparents had six children, so there was a ton of family, young and old, around all the time for me to soak up some wisdom from, or on rare occasions, the opposite—to learn how *not* to behave, bless their misguided hearts! Without a doubt, my mother was always my greatest female role model. And coming in a close behind were both of my grandmothers. They were vastly different from one another, but they were both very strong women. My late grandmother on my dad's side, Loretta Kirby, was a devout churchgoer. My grandfather passed away when I was about a year old, and Grandma Kirby never remarried. She wouldn't even consider it. After my grandfather died, she moved into town to be within walking distance of the church. She went to church every single day and grew flowers in her yard that she took to the church to decorate the altar. Grandma Kirby knew the birthdays not only of her children but also of her fifty-six grandchildren and great-grandchildren. She was extraordinary.

So was my grandmother Arlene Jockheck, on my mother's side. When she and Grandpa J. were first married and had young children, they struggled to raise their family on the farm. They didn't have much money, and their church pastor came to them demanding they tithe 10 percent. He said if they didn't have money to do that (which they didn't), the church would take their chickens instead. My grandfather refused to comply, knowing that the chickens were all he had to feed his family.

Understandably, my grandparents never went back to church after that. Later, they ran a bar in Spencer, South Dakota. They hosted exciting Christmas gatherings, drank alcohol, played cards, and told dirty jokes all over the place! This was dramatically different from the holidays with the Kirbys. But lo and behold, later in life (after turning ninety), Grandma Jockheck has started going back to church and has re-found her faith. I need to mention, too, that my Jockheck grandparents fostered another forty children in addition to raising their own six kids. Some of those foster children still keep in touch with my grandmother, today.

I grew up appreciating that these two worlds of my grand-parents—which were so different—produced beautiful, generous people who would do anything for anybody. My grandmothers and my own dear mother taught me how to care for others through their distinctive approaches to nurturing. They are at the very top of my Role Model Roster.

Because of these three authentic women who bravely, unapolo-getically, claimed their space on this earth in their own ways—these strong role models who all found joy in working hard and opening their arms wide to others—the idea of home is very important to me. For me, home has always been that safe place, a landing spot I can count on. It's not a physical building, and it's not a certain person (although obviously having your family there as your safety net is always a big part of it). But to me, home is where I can go and be myself, as my mother and grandmothers were truly themselves. I can be frustrated, angry, happy, or sad and know that I will be loved and supported.

The idea of home is so important to me that I try to make my work environment a nurturing, safe space for my employees and for our clients. I want everyone to feel free to express themselves without any judgment and to feel that they matter. I wouldn't mind someday winding up on someone else's Role Model Roster as an example of someone who celebrates acceptance for all.

I talk a lot about nurturing, but my fierce Irish dad taught me how to be tough and use my head in a crisis. He grew up on a family farm in rural South Dakota. As the baby of the family with four older brothers and one sister, he was taught the same philosophy of independence and fearlessness that he passed down to us kids. When it was time for him to learn how to ride a bicycle, his siblings took him to the top of a hill on a gravel road, put him on a bike, pushed him, and said, "Figure it out." He learned how to swim when they threw him into the middle of the pond and laughed as they walked away. In his family, you learned to swim, or you drowned. I'm kidding, but I'm not—I mean, surely they would have gone back to rescue him! But luckily, it never got that far. Dad learned how to swim right then and there.

When I learned to drive, my dad took me out in his old pickup onto a frozen lake. He said, "You need to learn how to drive on ice, and you need to know how to maintain a vehicle on ice. So do it." (My mother never handled this rite of passage well. Dad went through it with all of my siblings.)

It was a scary lesson. Dad made me spin out in the middle of the lake, and while the truck was out of control, he reminded me not to step on the gas or the brakes. He said I should take my feet off the pedals completely. If I step on the gas or the brakes, either action would send me into a deadly tailspin.

The key, he told me, was to turn into the direction I was sliding. If we'd been on a real road heading toward a telephone pole or a ditch, he said I should turn the wheel toward it. If I turned the wheels away from the direction I was sliding, the vehicle would not only continue to spin but I'd amplify it, as well!

It felt counterintuitive to turn toward danger. I had to trust in my father's experience and that of countless other people who'd successfully used that driving technique before me. It took hard-core focus. But it sure paid off. My spin stopped. And I knew that I'd be ready next time I lost control.

That day with Dad, I learned that instead of looking away, I needed to face my challenges head-on and not just on a slippery road. I also learned that preparation was a big part of success.

Letting go and having faith in yourself—taking on the hard stuff and overcoming your fear—aren't easy for most of us. Yet it's our job as caring parents, employers, colleagues, and friends to encourage others to navigate their challenges, too. I thought I knew how to do this. I raised my kids with permission to fail, the same way my parents raised me. I'd say, "Go out and play—if you're bleeding or dying, then come back home and we'll take care of it."

But it's funny how I thought twice about that way of thinking when I became a grandmother. My second granddaughter has cerebral palsy, and while she's impacted in all four of her limbs, she's a pretty determined little girl. If she wants to do something, she's going to do it. When she was three and experiencing a lot of weaknesses in her arms and hands, my boyfriend at the time and I took her to the playground. She wanted to climb up a ladder to get to a platform so she could go down the slide. And I thought, "Oh my goodness, she can't do this. She can't do this. Her hands and arms are not strong enough to hold her up."

So I was standing under her, holding her rear end as she climbed up. And my boyfriend said, "You need to let her do it. She can do it." I replied, "But she's going to fall!" And he answered, "Then she'll get back up. Back off and let her do this. She'll be prouder of herself for doing it than if you pushed her up that ladder."

And so I did. I let go, and she made it! It was scary for me, and for her, too. But the joy on her face when she got up there, I'll never forget it.

Having grandchildren has reminded me that despite all the risks I've taken and challenges I've met face-to-face, I can still be beset by fears. What I've learned over the years is to take a deep breath, look up to remind myself that God is watching over me, and then I sit with that particular fear, pray about it, examine it, and work with it. Eventually, I can put it in its proper place. I've reframed the old saying, "God does not give us more than we can handle" to a more appropriate version, "God does not give us more than He can handle."

I also do something that might seem lighthearted and silly, but it works like a charm to bring back my adventurous spirit. I had an opportunity to attend a women's conference with Lisa Nichols (https://motivatingthemasses.com/) shortly after starting my entrepreneurial journey. She taught me the importance of "Yes. YES!" When I'm in the car by myself on a day I'm not feeling my most courageous self, I yell, "Yes. YES!" And I'll think about what I'm hesitant to do at that time. Sometimes those things pile up: I'm reluctant to try a new workout; I'm nervous about buying the next building I have been dreaming about adding to my business; I'm not crazy about learning ballroom dancing.

So I'll yell, "Yes. YES, Korena!" as many times as I need to, the first yes for the situation and the second yes for me. It always makes me feel bolder. I usually laugh because it's funny to yell at yourself out loud, and I often get sideways looks from those around me or in the car next to me.

We do what we can to work around our natural human foibles and get to where we want to go, and sometimes, the unsophisticated, crazy things we do to pump ourselves up highlight how very human we are. And that's OK.

## THOUGHTSHOT

Life isn't about striving for shiny superhero status. That's an impossible ideal. An ordinary life—like my own, the beginnings of which I described to you in this chapter—can create a wonderful foundation for a person to do extraordinary things.

*What is wonderfully ordinary about you? How has that helped you do something extraordinary? And how can you make the best of both kinds of traits?*

I went from being a timid, small-town single mom to becoming a successful, nationally recognized businesswoman who gets to make tough decisions every day.

We are all flawed. But the secret to being a successful human is *attitude*. Do you have a generosity of spirit? Do you have grit? Do you have curiosity? Do you have a sense of adventure?

Before I graduated high school, my family and I moved eighteen times, sometimes just across town and sometimes across the country. New territory, new home. We had it down to a science: packing cardboard boxes, saying goodbye to next-door neighbors, figuring out the new school situation. As a result, I developed the bold mindset of an explorer, braving the unknown, digging deep down for the pluck and inventiveness I'd need to adjust to our new territory.

I look back now and see that exploration has been a major theme throughout all my life. I'd even call it a facet of my philosophy of looking up. Maybe I won't change the course of human history, like the great explorers we've all studied in school, but as I take one step forward and two steps back, then a great big zigzag leap ahead—however, I get there!—I can slowly but surely change the world around me. I can change my neighborhood, my work environment, and my family's trajectory.

Having a sense of purpose like that—and really believing I can make a difference—is an empowering feeling. But it didn't come easy, my getting to this place of clarity, confidence, and commitment. Sometimes I see only the promise of something, a glimmer, and I want to chase after it. Many times, I've hesitated, fearful of the next step. Questioning the right path. But, more often than not, I move. I take calculated risks (and occasionally impulsive ones).

Well, sometimes I catch whatever it is, and sometimes my adventure is a bust. That's life. But I never regret my choices, and I cannot change the past. I learn from them and know that there are very few things that we do in this world that we can't change. You always have options, even if you don't see them right there in front of you at this moment.

Being an adventurer is scary, and sometimes I'm nervous and afraid. But I do it. I risk leaving my safe space, and I get messy, and I fail. But eventually successes start building, and before I know it, I'm on a roll. I'll hit another snag. I trip and fall. I might rest there a moment, but I always get back up, brush off the dirt, and move forward.

Are you an adventurer in your life? What positive characteristics do you share with famous explorers, real or fictional, whom you admire? How can you incorporate those traits, or virtues, more into your everyday life?

## "You Betcha"s

1. You betcha you should indulge your curiosity and imagination. That's celebrating you and discovering why you are meant to be here. Should you cultivate grit? You betcha. Give yourself permission to do bold things you thought were out of your reach. Be an adventurer! Yes. YES!

2. You betcha you should use your head. Literally look up through the day. Be aware of your surroundings. Figuratively, pull back the camera on your life and look at each situation in context. Stay grateful. Take advantage of opportunities as they present themselves.

3. You betcha seeking out a mentor is a great idea. Make sure they're an expert you have good reason to trust.

# Establishing Your Life Goal

*A woman is like a tea bag.*
*You never know how strong she*
*is until she gets into hot water.*

**—ELEANOR ROOSEVELT**

"**K**orena, what's the answer?"

I looked up from my math textbook to the high school teacher waiting expectantly at the overhead projector beaming numbers and letters on a whiteboard behind him. He'd caught me. I'd been lost in thought about what my infant daughter was doing at that very moment. Was she sleeping? Was she hungry? I worried that the diaper rash she'd developed from a food sensitivity I'd recently discovered was getting worse. I hoped the caregiver was changing her frequently.

Solving an algebra equation was the last thing on my mind. But the truth was, I needed to pay attention. For my baby. I wanted to leave high school with a diploma. And then I wanted to go to college. My daughter deserved a mother who could take care of her without anyone else's help.

So I inched up a little in my seat and delivered the right answer, glad that math came easily to me. And when I left school that day, I ignored the gaggle of seniors talking by the lockers about what parties they were going to attend that weekend.

"I can't wait to get out of this place," one kid said. "I'm ready for freedom."

Freedom. I no longer had the same options he had. He didn't have a child to worry about yet. But I didn't pity myself. It was what it was, and I wouldn't have traded my position for his. No, as soon as I saw my daughter's face in the delivery room, my whole world grew bigger and brighter. I had a purpose that was noble and true: to be an amazing mother to her. And nothing would stop me from my goal. Nothing.

Looking up at the teacher that day, in those few seconds, my life goal crystallized for me. I faced where I was currently—a single mom in high school, a very awkward situation—and I committed to my plan to graduate. Nowadays I call that memory my supreme "Hashtag Goals" moment. Hashtags weren't even a thing when I was in high school, so in honor of that less tech-y time, I imagine the phrase in my head written out without the actual hashtag symbol attached. And whenever something means a lot to me, I think, "Hashtag Goals."

I know it's a gimmicky expression, but our brains love to play along with the shorthand tricks we use to move ourselves into the spheres of change and growth. I save my Hashtag Goals habit for the really big things. They become seared onto my heart, onto my very soul! However, when I get a chance, I also commit those goals to paper, usually a notebook on my desk. But I have a friend with a personalized online journal because she prefers typing her Hashtag Goals on a keyboard over writing freehand.

There's nothing wrong with writing your goals down in more than one place, so I usually also have them saved on my computer and a sticky note on my bathroom mirror. I have another friend who rips words and pictures out of old magazines and collages her Hashtag Goals on a framed poster she keeps in her closet so that she can see them every day. Sometimes she'll make Pinterest pages for her Hashtag

Goals when she doesn't have a stack of magazines to inspire her—her vision board.

Whatever you do, just remember: people who claim their goals out loud and focus on them reach them more often than people who do not write or speak their goals.

By the way, there's no shame in having to recommit to a Hashtag Goal every single day if that is what it takes. We are imperfect. It's natural to get distracted by the daily challenges of life as we confront outright obstacles to moving forward, which is why stopping to reclaim our goals is so important. It energizes us when we assert our purpose. It reminds us of our motivation for creating that goal, too. To this day, I think of the seventeen-year-old young mother I was and her burning desire for financial independence when I have to pick up the phone and make an intimidating call to a potential client I really want to work with.

But it's common knowledge that many people are hesitant to state their life goals. It's funny, none of us mind making simple goals part of our lives, like going to the grocery store. Beforehand, we might even consult our favorite recipes website and then create a list of foods we want to buy. Or we're happy to follow the usual sequential list in our heads outlining how we get to work in the morning: turn off the alarm, take a shower, get dressed, eat breakfast, jump in the car, and walk into the office ready to go hard with that day's requirements. Those are two perfectly fine, necessary goals for most of us—grocery shopping and getting ourselves to work—and both come with a map of steps we follow without even thinking.

Yet, when it comes to *big* life goals, many people get nervous contemplating them and saying what they're striving for, much less planning a way to get there. Instead, we're sidelined by questions like: *What if I fail at achieving my dream? Will I feel like a loser? Will other people mock me?* No one likes to be embarrassed. No one likes to fail.

But I believe those are only secondary rationalizations for not stating one's goals. The primary reason we don't is because (1) we might not have a plan to get ourselves to that goal, and (2) whatever plan we eventually follow (if we take the time to strategize) will set us off on a path that will likely alter our lives forever.

Change can be exciting. But scary, too. Often, real drama is involved when we make big pledges to ourselves and the world. Sometimes we make these decisions to commit to something as a result of an event we never anticipated. Surprises are not always fun. They're disconcerting, and so we delay responding, sometimes until it's too late and our best options have dried up. However the change enters our lives, we're best served by focusing and facing it decisively.

It's easy to say. Often hard to do. However we approach the situation, we are challenged to become our best selves, while we are sometimes confused and afraid. So it's no wonder these pivotal moments of clarity about our Hashtag Goals are branded into our psyches.

Everything changed for me when I made the momentous choice to become a single mother. And yes, several decades later, I can still tear up recalling when I found out I was pregnant as a teenager. Echoes of intense memory come back: the fear, the pressure, the shame, the loneliness, and then the sheer joy at meeting this new little person entrusted to my care and my determination to always protect and nurture her.

As I said earlier, that frightened, impassioned, young woman is still a part of who I am today. Some thirty years later, she has her role in influencing decisions I make. I will never forget her. I don't want to. My seventeen-year-old self might have been confused and scared, but she was also brave, loving, and visionary. She set me on an unexpected path I've fully embraced, turning me toward making the best decision of my life: to bring up my newborn on my own—not on welfare and not beholden to my parents, her uninvolved bio-dad, and my friends. And I would accomplish my goal by becoming a successful, independent businesswoman.

Had I known how difficult it was going to be to get from Point A—which involved heavy reliance on my parents to help me through the initial, turbulent phases of motherhood—to Point B, where I am today, well able to support my family and also skilled at helping my employees support theirs, I might have been too intimidated to set out on that path.

Like most teen mothers, I didn't plan on having a child in high school. I was young and naïve. The breakup with my boyfriend, which happened before I knew I was pregnant, was ugly. We'd met in high school, but he was two years older and enlisted in the Army. I didn't see a future for us because I didn't love him the way you should when you're in a long-term, committed relationship.

I waited to tell him the bad news, choosing to reveal my feelings at the end of his visit home for Christmas my junior year. I didn't want to face hurting him with the truth until the last possible moment. I learned a hard lesson then: burying your head in the sand is never a healthy thing to do.

## THOUGHTSHOT

Face the truth as soon as you know it. The hard stuff gets harder when you ignore it.

*When have you stuck your head in the sand and paid the price for doing so later? Is there anything in your life right now that you are ignoring that you should really be examining?*

Proof of that came not quite a month later. I wasn't feeling well. My mother came to me and said, "Do you think maybe you're pregnant?" I said, "What are you talking about? That's ridiculous." And she replied, "Hmm. I think maybe we should go get a test."

At the time, I had no idea how she knew. It did not cross my mind for a second. When she took me to the doctor for the pregnancy test, there were so many emotions—the fear, the shame, and the uncertainty that come with becoming a young mother without a partner. How would this pregnancy impact my future?

My ex-boyfriend offered to marry me. But once again, I asserted that I need to marry only a man I thought would make a great life partner for me, later, when I was older and more able to handle such a huge responsibility. On the heels of that declaration, he said he was washing his hands of the entire situation. He wasn't interested in being a father to our child when I didn't want to be with him.

> Is there a goal in your future that you can envision reaching?
>
> How will it be physically manifested in your life?

So after talking to my devout Catholic parents, I made the decision that was right for me: to have my baby and live at home until I got my high school diploma. My Hashtag Goal of becoming financially independent meant that a high school diploma wouldn't suffice. I was going for an advanced degree, too.

It was humbling to know I couldn't do it alone at first. I was seriously dependent on my family to help me get through that initial stormy time. I clung to the blessing that my parents were. If it weren't for my mother and father, I'd have been in a terrible position. At age seventeen, I didn't qualify for any state or federal financial aid. I couldn't get WIC. I couldn't get food stamps.

I arranged with the high school to attend the final required courses from eight o'clock to eleven o'clock in the morning. I put my daughter in daycare and worked after school in a discount clothing store, where I made enough to pay for that childcare and buy diapers and formula. My mom picked up my daughter when she got off work, which meant my daughter didn't have to be in daycare full time.

Throughout this period, I saw clearly that with state laws as they were, if I hadn't had Mom and Dad's help, I would never have been able to support my daughter on my own. The knowledge that I was entirely dependent on others to scrape by strengthened the desire to be completely financially independent. I was determined to find a livelihood that would give me the freedom to make my own choices; I knew I needed to go to college.

Being a single mother in high school also stirred the occasional feeling of shame in me, although 100 percent of the time I was thrilled and grateful to have my precious daughter. My family had given me a pass for my lack of maturity with the ex-boyfriend—after all, my beautiful baby girl had been the result, and we were all blessed by her presence in our lives. But plenty of other people judged me poorly for where I'd landed. According to prevailing wisdom, I had thrown away all sorts of the usual opportunities to be successful.

I'll never forget the moment my daughter was born. I couldn't wait to hold her in my arms and gaze on her little face. However, the maternity ward nurses presumed, without asking, to take her away post-delivery before I could even see her. Clearly biased against me because I was a teen, they explained later that they wanted to give me an opportunity to make a clear-headed decision about whether or not to put her up for adoption. Their reservations about my suitability as a mother made me that much more determined to give my baby daughter—with her rosebud mouth and sweet button eyes that pierced my soul and filled my heart with love—the life she deserved.

Shame dominated much of my early adulthood. Thanks to Dr. Brené Brown, author of *Daring Greatly* and *I Thought It Was Just Me*, I understand better what it is. She says shame is often mixed with the concept of guilt. Guilt can be useful when we employ it about wrong steps we've taken; it can help us return to a healthier path. I certainly used the regret—coupled with guilt—to propel me in a better direction.

But what is shame if it's not the same as guilt? Dr. Brown says shame is essentially a fear of disconnection. When we question whether we're worthy to belong or be accepted anymore, that's shame.

As I walked down the halls of my high school and watched my peers leading normal adolescent lives, the insidious feeling of not belonging—of feeling like an imposter—would overcome me. The other kids, understandably, couldn't relate to my life as a single mother. Looking back, I realize that the shame I harbored was often dependent on how tired or frustrated I was feeling at the time. Shame tends to gain entry when we aren't feeling our best, physically, emotionally, or spiritually.

It saddens me to recall those low moments. Of course, I was worthy of acceptance! I had every right to go to high school and not apologize for my circumstances to anyone.

I'm happy to say that shame was not able to take a deep hold on me when I was a young, single mother, although it had plenty of opportunities to do so in a small town. My parents must have recognized this, so once a week they insisted on babysitting so that I could hang out with my high school friends. I was able to stay connected, even if it meant it was in a different way. I regrouped and reframed. So did my friends. We all adjusted to the new life I was creating.

I grew stronger the more connected I felt. I would not let anyone shame me into silence or invisibility anymore, the way those delivery room nurses did. I stood my ground, which meant not apologizing for keeping my daughter. I risked being vulnerable to the slings and arrows others might direct at me—both strangers and acquaintances—for the choice I made.

I had to be brave. I had to stay in that space. I would stay connected, not just for me but for my baby girl, too. I never wanted her to grow up thinking she was anything but the best thing that had ever happened to me or to the world she would inhabit and shape.

# 

The bottom line is that *nurturing connection stops shame.* I have never forgotten that lesson. I call it the number one Shame Buster.

I didn't realize it at the time, but as a pregnant teen, and then as a single mom, I was employing Shame Busters, and so were my parents and friends, to help me love myself and to find the courage to stay connected. When we remind ourselves we're worthy of love and acceptance by the world—and ourselves—we're using Shame Busters.

Yours might be different from mine. Maybe you make an effort to look people in the eye and smile and nod—acknowledging them as a small act of positive affirmation. Maybe you compliment strangers or show people that they are accepted for who they are. However you approach this, I have found some commonalities between all our Shame Busters, whatever they are: *Every Shame Buster takes us right back to love and connection.* That's it.

One of my Hashtag Goals is to toss Shame Busters around wherever I go. I fling them into big and small gatherings like confetti at a parade. I don't want anyone to feel they aren't worthy of acceptance of belonging. We need to celebrate who we are. Yes, we are imperfect. We are broken. But that's what makes us human. And that loving self-acceptance inspires us to reach higher, to become better, and to encourage others to do the same.

For me, one favorite Shame Buster is reminding myself of my family. I'll look at photos of my hardworking grandparents and parents, decency and generosity etched into their expressions, and I feel proud to have descended from their ranks. Or I'll text one of my children. They always let me know I'm loved through little gestures like asking for advice or sharing something that happened during their day. Or I'll call a girlfriend and vent without worrying what she'll think of me—because we are that close, and she loves me at my best time and my worst.

Often, I turn to the greatest example of love that I know—my God. Nothing takes my shame away more than realizing I am loved fiercely by my Creator, who doesn't ever—*ever!*—make mistakes. The one who made me perfect in his eyes and knows what is in store for me.

I refuse to let shame win, so I stay intentional to making the world a better place, whether that's at home, the office, or in my community. I don't allow myself to be sidelined. Every day I see the results of my putting in my best effort. I am proud of how much I have accomplished in my family, my career, and in my neighborhood, as a caring friend, as a happy face in the grocery store line, or on a local charitable board.

In the game of life, I win when I protect myself with Shame Busters. Shame doesn't stand a chance. It slinks away. I wish the same outcome for you. Remind yourself all the time that you're worthy of belonging.

Yes, indeed, I was learning great lessons about life as a teen mom. I was proud to become stronger and wiser. But as we all know, we never stop growing. Stuff keeps happening, good, bad, and indifferent—and as I said before, sometimes it takes us by surprise, which means we really have to be on our A-game.

My Big Hairy Audacious Goal (BHAG) of going to college meant that I had to plan for it. So I started going through the process of evaluating the following: *Where can I go? Where should I go? How can I pay for this? What kind of financial aid is available to me?*

I chose a private college in Sioux Falls, 40 miles from home. I found a little basement apartment and a close-by daycare. To live independently and attend classes full time, the days were long. A typical day would start at six o'clock in the morning where I worked as a fry cook at a taco place before classes. Then I'd go to class, clean houses between classes, and be a waitress in the evening. I'd pick up my daughter after my last shift and take her home for a few hours of play time before putting her to bed and sitting down to my homework.

At eighteen, I became eligible for government benefits, but I kept losing them. I found out quickly that when you work your butt off to make money, you get less and less support from the state. Not only that, when I got my very first child support check—two days before my daughter's first birthday—it was only fifty dollars. I knew my ex-boyfriend's wages in the military were being garnished for more than that. So when I called and asked about it, the government worker said, "You owe the state money because we've been supporting you for the last several months, and so you have to pay us back. We're keeping the child support check, and we're just giving you what you need based on how much money you're making."

It was the craziest thing. Extremely frustrating, too, when I was simply trying to do the right thing and work to support myself as best as I could in my circumstances. Instead, the government punished my initiative by withholding state benefits and financial support.

Another crushing eye-opener for me occurred when I went to pick up my daughter from the first daycare in Sioux Falls I had enrolled her in. It was a home-based operation set up in a garage but really nicely done. I got there earlier than usual one afternoon. The daycare operator and her son were sitting outside drinking beer—and there were no kids.

Alarmed at those Miller Lites in their hands and the utter quiet, I said, "Where are the children?"

The operator said, "Oh, we put them to bed. It's seven o'clock."

I was getting more and more nervous. "Well, where are they sleeping?"

Her son said, "We put them in the house to go to bed at night." And he explained that they had a basement, and—

I stopped listening, turned around, and walked right into the house. They followed me, both of them saying, "No, no! You don't go down there. We'll get her."

*Down.* There was no way they'd be able to watch the kids stuck in a basement while they were outside drinking beer.

I started to shake all over, but I ignored their demands that I turn around. Instead, I marched down some cellar stairs and found my daughter in an unfinished room. Nine kids on a little area rug. Three were in a pack-and-play. The smallest of the three was my daughter. There were no blankets. No pillows, other than what they each had brought with them. There were no lights on. Half of the kids were crying.

I grabbed my daughter and said to the operator, "You will never see this child again."

I walked out and sobbed all the way home. I cried when I pulled in the driveway, and I cried when I carried my sweet baby girl downstairs to the cozy, finished basement I lived in—what a difference from the ugly, dark holding space at the daycare. I didn't leave my apartment for three days and went through a whole box of Kleenex wiping away my tears.

Looking back on that crisis, I realize it was one of those moments—one of those pivotal moments—when you question what the heck you're doing. I couldn't believe I had done this to my child! Terrible thoughts went through my head. I doubted my parenting skills. How could I have misjudged that daycare operator so badly?

I'm very much the mothering type with a servant's heart. I love to take care of people. So I was absolutely devastated that I'd failed to deliver on my promise to my daughter, to care for and protect her at all times. It made me question every decision. Should I be in school? Should I be living in Sioux Falls? Should I be working?

My daughter had changed my life, my feelings, and my priorities. Her safety was so much more important than my own personal well-being. Maybe I should drop out, move home, and give up on being independent. I could stay with the folks. Lower my expectations for myself.

I eventually pulled myself together and left my apartment. I still felt that I couldn't think straight. I was too upset. So I had serious talks with people I trusted. At that point, I was so driven by emotion and felt so close to the situation that I worried I couldn't make good decisions. I relied on my inner circle for encouragement and advice.

And yes, those heart-to-hearts helped. A lot. My head cleared. I decided it was too soon to give up on school. I talked to the family who lived upstairs, and they were able to recommend a really good daycare for my daughter. So I started my life up again, a little wiser this time. And I forgave myself for making a mistake about that first daycare situation in Sioux Falls.

#

While it is perfectly natural to feel alone/stupid/embarrassed when we get ourselves into tight corners, we cannot allow shame or fear to keep us there. When we feel shame or humiliation, we tend to become afraid to ask for advice or assistance from other people. We need to have the courage to ask for advice, ask for help, to persevere, and to move out of the negative space.

Remember: whatever it is you are experiencing, you are not the only one—many have been in that exact position before you, and others will be there after you. Don't waste time blaming yourself for it. Seek a solution. Having a heart-to-heart conversation is one of my all-time favorite strategies for navigating difficulties. Actually, I call them Heart-to-Hearts in capital letters. That word, in my view, is a literal representation of who we all are: a string of connected hearts.

I believe we are all invisibly connected. Your pain is mine. My pain is yours. We are all from the same one who created us. Sharing our wisdom, our caring, and our love is the most natural thing we can do when one of us is in crisis.

Do you have someone in your life whom you trust will listen to your problem and have your best interests at heart? I hope so. It is a blessing, so keep those relationships thriving. Thank those people often and support them back.

However, if you don't feel you have anyone to talk to when you need a confidant, take a moment to look around at people close by. Heart-to-Hearts can happen between strangers. Some of the best advice I've ever been given was from strangers I met at conferences, walking in the park, or on an airplane. Help is out there. Go to a pastor, or to a therapist, or to your local police station. Tell someone you need assistance. Knock on your neighbor's door. Find a helpful resource on the internet.

I promise you, if you keep an open heart, you will eventually be rewarded for having the kind of faith that trusts in the goodness of people. You won't regret reaching out for help, even though it's scary. Vulnerability is terrifying, but it's the only way to create a real connection and breakthrough.

We have all been in trouble in some form or another, at some point in our lives. Let's remember that each of us suffers in some way, and let's stay aware of our capability to help our fellow humans and to receive help from them, too.

## "You Betcha"s

1. You betcha connection stops shame in its tracks.

2. Should I follow my gut instincts? You betcha, especially ones about your kids and loved ones. Ninety-nine percent of the time, your gut is right.

3. You betcha change means growth. We sometimes try to avoid change because it can involve stress or drama. But if it gets you closer to your Hashtag Goals, remind yourself you can handle it.

# Connect with Your Fellow Humans

*I never dreamed about success.*
*I worked for it.*
**—ESTÉE LAUDER**

I was a young single mother opening her eyes to a buzzing alarm clock and looking up to gauge the weather from the small block of light that streamed through my basement apartment window. Occasionally, I could see shoes padding by. The bottom half of a bike tire. A pregnant momma cat mincing along the gravel, her belly swaying.

It was time to start another long day. My baby slept nearby, so I never felt alone, but I definitely felt lonely in the busy community that comprised Sioux Falls. I had to be my own taskmaster, advisor, and best friend. I didn't have time for typical college relationships, either social or academic, of a traditional college student. In addition to my studies, I was too busy being a working mom.

I fed and clothed us both; took my daughter to daycare; went to work; attended classes so I could earn my diploma; headed to a different job; picked up my little one from daycare; loved on her as much as I could at dinner, bath time, and before bedtime; studied at my tiny kitchen table; and then started it all over again the next day. I was doing what I had to do to make ends meet and move toward my dream of financial independence, one step at a time.

It was the best plan I could come up with for my life. Steady wins the race. I clung to that fable about the hare and the turtle. By golly, I was the turtle in this race to success, and sometimes that fact drove me nuts—I wanted to get where I wanted to be immediately!—but the wisdom of the tale also calmed me down. "It's OK," I'd tell myself when I finally turned off the light at night. "It's OK. Take the long view, Korena. Look up."

More often than not, this attitude worked for me. My ancestors were farmers. They had to wait on a crop to grow. Many steps must be taken, patience shown.

But there came a day when my stoicism and confidence were severely tested. My vision for my future blurred—yet again. I pondered if what I felt was akin to what one of my grandparents or great-grandparents might have felt when they planted a crop and a tornado or locusts swept through and wiped it out before it could be harvested. I wondered if I was doing the right thing, making the right choices. I wondered if I was crazy to pursue my dreams and if I truly had it in me to reach them.

It was a Friday afternoon. I was exhausted, but my heart lifted when I collected my pay and drove to the daycare to pick up my daughter. But my good mood dissolved when the daycare operator gave me the bill for the week, and I saw that I owed her three dollars more than what I'd earned in the past seven days. I literally sat on her porch and cried. I was thinking, "I can't buy groceries this week. I can't put gas in my car. And I still owe her more money that I don't even have."

That day was crushing to my soul. I wondered what I was missing—how did people do this? What was I doing wrong? What did I need to change? I hated asking anybody for help. I didn't want to ask my parents for money, and I shouldn't have had to. I was working two jobs and doing everything I could to better myself. So why was I still struggling so hard?

No doubt the good lady had seen despairing single mothers like me before. She wasn't fazed. She said not to worry a bit about the three dollars; God bless her. Her kindness helped me in that moment. She reminded me that connection was the key to survival in this world. Love. Generosity of spirit. United hearts. An almost infinite chain of them had come before me and would extend into the future long after I was gone, my daughter's among them.

## THOUGHTSHOT

I'd forgotten about togetherness. I was so used to fighting forward on my own, like a tenacious jungle warrior using a machete to slash through scary undergrowth to get to her safe place, oblivious to the fact that nearby was a road that led there—if only she'd slow down, breathe, and look.

*Can you think of a time when the answer was right there in front of you but you were too isolated, anxious, or hyper-focused to see it? What happened? Did you find the solution in time or not? What strategies can you take forward to help you the next time you get caught in a similar pattern? Could those strategies help others, too? If so, who would you most want to pass your newfound wisdom on to if they're seeking your advice?*

I am a very stubborn person. Sometimes that's good; sometimes it's not. I vowed on my daycare operator's porch step to remember that asking for help was not a bad thing. I would do better if I admitted my vulnerability—not worse. I already knew this! But in the heat of the moment, in the middle of a crisis, it was difficult for me to open my heart to receiving help.

After that daycare financial scare, I still had to think about how I was going to continue on my chosen (but extremely rocky) path. From then on, I would try to see my roadblocks as opportunities to connect.

I pushed on with more awareness of my surroundings. I was honest with other people about my need to make more money, and as a consequence, I was able to add more waitressing shifts and do odd jobs for extra cash. I kept my shoulder to the grindstone and refused to quit. Meanwhile, my daughter, being so small, was none the wiser about my struggles. Luckily, by the time she was big enough to remember things, I was out of extreme financial crisis mode. I'm proud that I was able to protect her from that sort of stress. I'm proud that I made it through that desperate time. I learned some huge lessons, and my faith in God grew stronger. He'd said in the New Testament that if He could make the lilies of the field beautiful, He could surely take care of my needs. And He did, in so many ways.

Persevering in the face of doubts might seem silly to some. It's like standing in the surf with waves hitting you in the face over and over. Yeah, you look kind of goofy as you struggle to maintain your balance. But you start to get acclimated. You learn which muscles to tense, how to dig in your heels, when to pinch

Is there any challenge confronting you now that you're scared by?

Can you learn to work with it instead of blocking it?

List three positive ways you can grow if you invite this "wave" to interact with you!

your nose shut, and where to look for the next big wave. You go from *fighting* to *working with*, from *brittle* to *flexible*. And if you learn to look for fellow humans who can throw you a line if a riptide takes you by surprise—you will expand the boundaries of your heart. By receiving, you will learn how to give.

In the blur of unending challenges as a student, mother, and worker in Sioux Falls, I grew up and I reached out, opening up opportunities for myself, sometimes without even realizing I was doing so. Here's an example: through a very serendipitous class I took because I didn't know what other class to enroll in for the required credit I sought, I discovered the direction I wanted to move with my career: media ethics. A weight was lifted from my wandering heart, and in its place was a deep certainty that I belonged.

The truth is, when I went to college, I wasn't sure exactly what I wanted to study. Neither did I have any idea what job I wanted when I graduated. All I knew was that I planned to graduate. And there's not a thing wrong with that. Sometimes we have to set general targets. We might not be ready for anything more detailed in scope.

The beauty of college is that it supports people like me who aren't always sure what their passions are. College excels at helping us find our purpose because we're exposed to new things we might not have been aware of had we not gone to school. I just happened to take a college class about ethics in media, and that piqued my curiosity about the media in general. So I applied for an internship at a TV station and got the job.

*Wow* was my reaction once I started. I knew what I wanted to do, all of a sudden.

Take that, big waves! Or should I say thank you? I couldn't take credit for choosing that ethics class willy-nilly. It simply came flying down a random breaker and met me where I stood.

I call moments like that grace. I did nothing to earn it. It was a gift from my Higher Power. In his book *Grace: More Than We Deserve, Greater Than We Imagine*, Max Lucado says, "Grace is the voice that calls us to change and then gives us the power to pull it off."

I feel that. I rarely, if ever, hear that voice when I'm shut down, disconnected, so intent on my agenda that I lose sight of the fact that I'm not as in charge as I think I am. Gifts of grace show up when I'm at my most humble, which is a nice way to say when I'm so despondent or world-weary that I stop trying so hard to protect myself.

As a college sophomore working at the TV station, I wrote news captions and operated the cameras. Not very long afterward, I got into the advertising side. All this work experience was helping me fine-tune my big Hashtag Goal. I always knew I wanted to be financially independent so that I could take care of my daughter, but now I could add that I wanted to find a career in the media world. That specificity gave me more motivation to slog through the rest of the challenging times I faced in college as a single mom.

Fast-forward five years, and I had graduated college—hallelujah!—with a BA in mass communications/media studies. I was still at the TV station. I'd also gotten married. You could call me a single mom success story. My husband adopted my daughter, and we had another child.

But honestly?

Life keeps going. You meet a Hashtag Goal, and then what are you going to do? Quit? No. You see your goals evolve. I was financially independent but still living paycheck to paycheck, my husband and I making modest incomes that allowed us to pay for the basics of life, such as food, gas, housing, and childcare, which was a huge blessing. But gradually, I was learning that I wanted to be my own boss, too.

I still had a long way to go—about thirteen years—before that idea became so clear to me that I actually did something about it.

#

At age twenty-six, I was still clinging to my Hashtag Goal of becoming a successful businesswoman, but my position at the TV station had become emotionally draining. If this was success, I hated it. I had a boss who was not very understanding and verbally abusive. The job was literally sucking the life out of me. Making money mattered—and I was grateful for it—but I was finding out that the actual job matters just as much. I was going home feeling miserable and carrying that mood into my house. My family deserved better from me, but I didn't know what to do.

One thing that surprised me, too, was that I encountered other women who weren't supportive of their female colleagues. One was at the senior level. She'd say to me, "You're never going to understand this fully. So there's really no point in teaching you how to do it."

Ugh. I was always tempted to respond, "You have no idea what I'm capable of. I may not be the most brilliant person in the room, but I did pretty well in college, working three jobs, and being a single mom with a 3.8 GPA. I think that's pretty darned good."

But I didn't. I was too scared. I wish now that I could go back and tell her that! And suggest to her that supporting and encouraging other women would actually make her feel good.

Her attitude affirmed for me what I already suspected: that the media world was very much a man's world. If you've ever seen *Mad Men*, the TV show, I swear this industry was like that all the way through the '90s and well into the aughts and the 2010s. And I think the vestiges of that culture are still around. This industry can be brutal. Absolutely cutthroat. So to work with a woman who had that mentality was demoralizing for a young woman in her twenties who wanted to rise to the top of the business—because I still loved the work, in spite of the good ole boys' club mindset.

My unhappiness came to a head when I got food poisoning one night and called in sick the next morning, which didn't happen very often. If I was sick, I went to work. I only stayed out if one of my kids came down with something. But on this day, I called in because there was no way I could get in the car and drive there. Nor would the other employees want me around them. The symptoms of food poisoning are not pleasant, as most of us know. My timing was terrible, as often happens with illness. The boss was about to go on a two-week vacation. He said, "You don't have a choice. You have to get here because I need to get a lot of stuff done before I leave. I don't care what it takes, but you'd better be here by noon."

And so I was there by noon. I sat at my desk and typed my resignation letter. I handed it to him at five o'clock in the evening, knowing he was leaving the next morning for his vacation. And this time I spoke up. I said, "I'm turning this in now so I won't ever have to see you again."

I went home that night to tell my husband, and he was not happy that I'd quit. We definitely needed the income. I told him I'd figure something out but that I physically couldn't go back and work for that guy ever again.

From the outside looking in, my decision appeared impulsive, and I'll admit, occasionally I *will* make a quick decision. But if I do, it's because I feel a strong gut feeling, which I have come to trust. I'd tolerated my boss's lack of respect and caring until this food poisoning situation truly brought out the worst in him. At that point, I felt it imperative to leave the company. It wasn't false pride speaking in me, either. It was a recognition of my basic worth as a human being. I have my parents to thank for my "stand-up for yourself" attitude. When someone tries to treat me like a clump of dirt, I remind myself that they've got it all wrong—I'm a diamond!

You should believe you are, too.

I took a job in the mall selling mattresses, while I looked for work better aligned with my interests. I only had to sell mattresses for three months before I found a job in an agency as a media buyer and was able to get back into what I really loved. I would be purchasing advertising time for automotive dealer groups in large markets across the country.

The greatest part of it was, not only was I making more money, but I also loved my boss. She was an amazing mentor, a woman who taught me the entire industry. She was so good at bringing me into her deals and showing me the ropes. She equipped me to think critically and to be better at everything I did. She had high expectations, which she'd hold me to, but she treated me with respect and made it clear that she saw tremendous potential in me, which felt really good. She never raised her voice. She never cursed. She never called anyone names. She was professional about everything she did. Occasionally, she could be aggressive, but she always did it in such a way that people respected her and feared her a little bit. She used to say to me when I made a good deal, "Way to pound 'em!"

So, of course, I wanted to do my very best for her. To this day, I stay in touch with her because she meant so much to me. She showed me that a woman could be powerful in an industry dominated by men, and she could do it with kindness and by being supportive of other women. Anyone who's ever worked for her, I would hire in a heartbeat.

As much as I loved making deals with my wonderful boss, I left that agency when the owner hired a couple of ambitious men who came in acting as if they knew everything. I wasn't surprised. It's hard to find someone in this industry who isn't a little bit cocky, especially in the agency setting. However, these guys were demoralizing and demeaning in their approach. They'd ask you a question at ten o'clock in the morning, and if you didn't have the answer for them by eleven o'clock, they'd come right out and say you didn't know what you were doing, so they would do it themselves.

There were a lot of people there I could work with—we had some amazing employees, such as my boss with her warm caregiver's attitude. But these guys were ruthless. There were several days where I had to leave the office because I didn't want to sit and cry at my desk. I'd go somewhere else, cry, and come back. And the whole time, I'd think, "This is not what I want. I deserve better."

Remember, we're diamonds. Not clumps of dirt!

Sometimes you have to upset the apple cart if you truly want to assert your worth. It's risky, but what's worse: staying in a terrible situation in which you're not respected or cutting your losses and trying something new? Too often we stay in our ruts for fear of others casting judgment. But seriously, who cares? We have one life to live! I refuse to waste any of mine being undervalued.

One time when I left the office because I didn't want to cry at my desk, I went to my mom and dad's house nearby. I searched in the phone book for ad agencies and started calling all of them to ask if they were hiring. I shared my credentials, and one of them said they actually were looking for people.

I know in fairy tales things turn out great pretty fast. But this was real life. The good news: I wound up leaving my job where the two obnoxious guys worked and taking a job at this agency. The bad news: the new place wasn't perfect, either. I saw a red flag at the interview, in fact. The human resources person should have been interviewing me, but it was the actual manager who did instead. She asked me if I planned to have any more kids because they would not hire me if I was going to go on maternity leave.

Wow. It was against the law for her to ask that question. Aside from that, I thought it was so strange that I'd met yet another female who'd judge another woman that way. We already had it hard enough entering this traditionally masculine business arena, didn't we? But things were so bad at the other job, I took this one anyway. The first couple of years were pretty rough just because of that female manager's negative attitude. But eventually she got fired for it. In front of some higher-ups, she went off on working women and how mothers should not be in the workforce. She said they should be home caring for their kids, and she couldn't stand it when people took maternity leave. Come to find out, a senior vendor attending the meeting had five children, and her husband was a stay-at-home dad! She didn't take kindly to that manager's assessment of mothers in the workforce.

I really loved working at that agency after that manager was let go, and I wound up staying there ten years. I learned a lot, and I have great respect for the people I worked with while I was there.

Over those ten productive, exciting years, I also recognized that working for other people had its drawbacks. But I still wasn't at the tipping point where I considered opening my own business. Ironically, my reasons for starting my own firm had everything to do with my being a mother who faced an impossible situation: having to choose between my family and my job.

Let's stop and chat right now about how difficult life can be for working mothers in general. If you're a man, you've probably already heard about these female-centric issues, but it never hurts to hear about them again because we still have a lot of unhappy working moms out there who need more understanding.

Granted, a little over twenty years have gone by since that female manager inappropriately asked me if I planned to get pregnant. I'm glad to say times have changed for the better. Even so, every working mother I've ever talked to has felt they're always having to choose between taking care of their loved ones and having a really successful career.

Does this sound familiar? You always feel you're torn in different directions. If you're not home when your kids need you, you're sure you're letting them down. But when you're home, people at work might need you, too.

I'm servant-driven and always want to be there to support other people. But I found while working for other people in my twenties and thirties, I was always disappointing someone. When you have a sick child and you suddenly can't go into work and do what you need to do that day, and there's a tight deadline, that's nerve-wracking. Conversely, if you have to stay late at work, and you can't go home and make dinner and help with homework, that's stressful, too. There's always the challenge of deciding what's the most important thing at that moment. Almost inevitably, you'll be upsetting somebody along the way.

Traditionally, men seem to attract all the warrior metaphors. But look what we go through as women. We are incredible fighters. We produce the babies. We see to the well-being of the children, whether we work outside the home or not. Women multitask their way through each day like fairy godmothers for a weary world in need of love and courage—but without the magic wands.

The agency I worked at for ten years was a phenomenal place, and they said they were a family-first and Christian organization. That was true for the executive team and the vice presidents. However, I'm sad to say that for the rest of us, it really wasn't. There weren't a lot of women there who had children because the environment didn't support the needs of working moms. Most of the men had wives who stayed home.

Slowly, I began to see that my biggest Hashtag Goal of becoming a successful businesswoman to support my family was not the ideal dream to have if it meant I also couldn't be the mother, wife, sister, friend, and daughter I wanted and needed to be. I had to figure out a way to have it all.

But was that possible?

I couldn't see a way out of my dilemma. Feeling trapped was a terrible feeling. It's not in my nature to stick with something that doesn't sit well with my soul and isn't right for my family.

It turns out the solution had been there all along. Answers often are, but sometimes we're not ready for them yet. And sometimes we just need a nudge. A serendipitous event catapulted me into the intimidating but exciting world of entrepreneurship. Yet had I not been preparing for it for years—without even realizing it—I never would have recognized the opportunity, much less made myself into the successful businesswoman I am now.

I'll talk about that more in the next chapter, but meanwhile, I want to offer a gentle suggestion for all the working moms out there. When you feel torn in different directions, when your spirit is weary, please give yourself a bit of grace. You deserve it. I promise, when you go easier on yourself, your Higher Power will hear you and support you.

For me, grace has several aspects to it, and I like to remember them by breaking the word down as an acronym:

## G—Gift Yourself with Forgiveness

This is self-explanatory but very hard to do. I want you to imagine yourself asking your best friend or daughter to forgive herself if she "messes up." Wouldn't you want them to? Of course, you would! Now bestow that same love on yourself. Forgive yourself for being human. If you forgot the cupcakes for your child's class, or if you missed a meeting, or if you can't be there when your loved one has a rough day, it's OK. That doesn't mean you don't care. It means you're overwhelmed.

## R—Remember You Are God's Masterpiece

*For we are God's masterpiece.*
*He has created us anew in Christ Jesus,*
*so we can do the good things he planned for us long ago.*
**EPHESIANS 2:10**

Blogger and podcaster Holley Gerth was inspired by this Bible verse when she said, "In a world full of pressure and expectations, it's easy to feel we should be all things to all people. But God says to us, 'I created you for a specific purpose. You are who you need to be to accomplish what I put only you on earth to do.'" We're not group projects. We're masterpieces who exist for the pleasure and purposes of the Artist. *We're invaluable and irreplaceable.* So let's breathe a sigh of relief today. We don't need to be all things to all people.

So remind yourself that you're a masterpiece! Especially when you least feel like one. For me, that's usually when I'm trying to please too many people at the same time. I don't need to please anyone but the God who made me.

## A—Axe the Extraneous and Streamline

We women have a hard time saying no. If you can't say it immediately—it gets stuck in your throat because you're worried you look uncaring—say, "Let me think about this, and I'll get back to you." Say that, at least! And then email or call later when you've worked up your courage.

Hopefully, you'll get to the point where you can simply say in the moment, "Thanks so much for thinking of me, and it sounds wonderful, but I have too much on my plate right now."

## C—Calendars Are Your Friend

I put everything on the calendar. Sometimes two. I have one on my phone and another on my desk. I'm very vocal with my family and work colleagues about my schedule and family calendar so they're not surprised by my level of commitments. I have found over the years that when you give people a heads-up and say, "For the next six weeks, I'm slammed," they are much more supportive than they would be if you simply stumble through those six weeks going back on promises that you thought you'd be able to keep regarding your presence at events, the dinner table, or the employee lounge.

## E—Embrace the Awkwardness

Life is messy. Good things never come easy. That's reality. It's OK not to be perfect. It's OK that it takes ten tries to succeed instead of one or two. Sweat and stumbles are part of the game. So are tears. Keep a box of tissues, some chocolate, and your sense of humor. I swear you will get through it all with flying colors!

# "You Betcha"s

1. You betcha we're going to hit frustrating stumbling blocks, but we don't have to take them on alone.

2. You betcha you deserve to be treated with respect. Period.

3. You betcha women who support other women, especially in a traditionally male environment, are heroes.

# Seizing New Opportunities

*I say luck is when an opportunity comes along and you're prepared for it.*
**—DENZEL WASHINGTON**

Every entrepreneur has their own reasons for starting up a business. They could be moved by the prospect of making more money, indulging their particular passion, taking the creative lead, or gaining autonomy over their direction in life—or a combination of the above. For me, it was about asserting my values, so I needed more control over my life. Not a motivator for me. I was doing well enough there. And I was already indulging my passion for marketing and had plenty of opportunities to lead with my creative vision. However, there was one big sticking point. I'm all about family, and it became very clear to me one day that my number one priority—to be the best parent possible—was at risk of being lost in the complex shuffle my life had become.

As a mother, I wanted and needed to be there more for my kids. And the only way I could make that happen while still working within the industry I loved was to start my own company. I don't mind telling you that I backed into this solution. Bump! And there I was, looking at a big dent in my life that I needed to fix. I could argue that the warning signs were there. It's easy to say that now. Hindsight is twenty-twenty, after all. But at the time, it felt like it wasn't until I "crashed" that I truly woke up to what was happening.

My son, Cole, thought my job was more important to me than he was. It was a hugely pivotal moment because it came when I thought things were going well in general. I'd been promoted at the agency and had taken on more and more responsibilities. At home, we were a busy family, but things were running smoothly. Yes, it was always super crazy trying to get the kids off to school, but I was thrilled to be there to support them (my husband was working nights, so he couldn't be there in the mornings). Cole was a freshman in high school that year and playing football. Their games were always at four o'clock. Cole wasn't the most organized kid in the world, and so we were both trying to find his pads and cleats and everything else he needed before he got on the school bus.

As he was running out the door with all his gear—mission accomplished!—I said, "okay, bud. I'll see you today at the game." My heart was full. These ordinary family moments were what I lived for. But I'll never forget that he stopped, as if he were surprised. "Are you *really* coming to my game today? You're going to make it?" he asked hopefully, and dare I say, a bit skeptically. "Of course, I'm going to be there," I reassured him. He replied without missing a beat: "I know you'll be late, Mom, but that's OK because I know your work is more important."

Then he took off for the bus, not even for a second realizing the impact his words had on me. I froze. I couldn't believe one of my kids thought my work was more important than he was. Never in a million years had I wanted to convey that message to Cole. And to make matters worse, there was that blanket statement, *Your work is more important.* What if he also assumed that jobs, in general, were more important than people?

Oh, my God. I was crushed. I wanted my children to feel loved. I wanted them to know that caring for their well-being was my top priority. I also wanted them to grow up believing that loving people mattered way more than pursuing worldly achievements.

I started crying, and I cried all the way into work. It was a thirty-five-mile commute, too, so by the time I got there, my eyes were swollen, my nose was stuffy, and I had a terrible headache. But nothing hurt worse than my heart. It was broken.

When my boss got in, I immediately went into his office and said, "Something has to change. I can't keep sacrificing my family for work. We need to hire somebody. *Something has to change.*"

My boss told me the company would work on it. They would figure it out.

I'm not a cynic. I'm a realist. I believed things would get better. Change is hard. Most people run from it.

Six months later, still nothing had evolved in my company's culture. So I went back into the boss's office and said, "Hey, I've talked to you about this. I need something to change because I'm not going to do another baseball or football season where I can't be at my kids' games, or I'm always showing up late. That's not in line with the values the company espouses, and it's not aligned with my values, either. So we have to do something about it. We need help. We need to hire more people."

"Yep, yep, yep," he said. "We're working on it. Just give us a little more time."

## THOUGHTSHOT

Folks, we can't wait for the world to change. We have to change ourselves.

*Can you think of an example in your own professional or personal life where you came to this realization? What did*

> *you do? Did you achieve your goal? If not, what happened next? Trace that journey of change and see where you put belief in yourself into action.*
>
> *Remember, it's never too late to keep trying. In fact, that's our job—to grow—until our dying day.*

I waited about another thirty days, and you guessed it—no progress had been made whatsoever on making family needs feel important at my workplace. I could have despaired. But I didn't. I chose to be proactive. I sat down and created a short list of what was next for me. If I could do anything, what would it be? Who would I want to work for? What would I want to be doing?

I knew that the digital space was where I wanted to be. I was determined to dig deeper and learn more about opportunities with online advertising. So I shortlisted a couple of companies and called them out of the blue. I said, "This is confidential, but I'm thinking about shopping my résumé. Would you be open to a conversation, or do you have anything available that would be appropriate for me?"

One company's owner said, "Absolutely. When can we talk?" And so over the course of the next month, we held several serious conversations. It took me another couple of months to turn in my notice and to tell my current agency that I was leaving. That moment took place in early July 2010. I went in and told the higher-ups that I couldn't stick around. I said I'd been asking them to change for almost a year, and nothing had. "I need to do what's right for my family," I said and felt a surge of power and calm asserting my values. I knew I was doing the right thing for me.

Six weeks later, after I'd trained someone to move in to take over my responsibilities, I left that agency. I'd been there a long time and had learned a lot. But listening to my heart was more important to me than professionally advancing there. I knew my heart would not lead me wrong. That deep knowledge came from having failed many times over already and picking myself back up again. I had done it before. I could do it again.

At the new company, I was working with truly gifted people. It was a small team of about five when I first started. They were knowledgeable and willing to experiment. I loved that attitude. They were brilliant innovators. But I also realized almost immediately that these creative geniuses weren't necessarily as great at running a business. Because of that, the business was not very stable.

I remember telling my husband, "I don't know that this job is going to last very long. I think if it lasts a year, we'll be fortunate. Based on what I'm making from them and based on what I'm saving by not having to commute all the time, I think we need to put as much money into savings as we can. Let's pay down as much debt as we can, too."

In other words, I wanted to shore up our finances and be prepared for my not having a job for a little while because I didn't know how long it would take me to find another job if this one ended.

On the first day of January 2011, the owner called and said he couldn't make payroll, was going on a six-month hiatus, and laying everyone off. He said I could go on unemployment and wait until they regrouped, or I could even go back to my previous agency. He encouraged me to do what was right for me and concluded with these devastating words: "Just know that we can't pay you."

I had been there only five months.

My instincts about the viability of that company had been right on target. There were a couple of weeks where I was wrapping stuff up for them and simply praying over what was next because I knew I couldn't go back to my old agency. It would send the wrong message to my kids, but it also wouldn't be good for my mental health. I couldn't go back to a place that didn't walk the walk when it came to upholding my values (and its professed ones) about family.

I was witnessing true grace in action, I believe, as I kept praying over what was next for me. Musing on the activities of the companies I'd worked for, I started thinking, *I can do that*. It had never occurred to me before to be my own boss. But I realized that I had built up a lot of skills in the past fifteen years of working for other people.

*I* could consult with agencies.

*I* could help them better integrate digital.

*I* could help them understand what capabilities were out there.

*I* could connect them with the right resources in order to work more efficiently, giving them access to tools that they didn't currently have access to.

It was like I was watching myself from the outside as I called up the owner of the company that had just let me go and said, "This is what I'm thinking, and I want to make sure it's OK with you because I don't want to cross any lines. I want to keep going on doing this work. But I want your blessing."

He said he was perfectly fine with my going out on my own in the same niche because—as he'd made it clear already—he was taking a massive step back.

My next question was, "I know that you have clients who need this work done. Since you're shutting down, do you mind if I call them and offer to continue to help them?"

"Absolutely," he said. "Go for it."

I felt the way you do when the starting gates open in front of the horses at the Kentucky Derby. Exhilarated. Tense. Grateful to be there. But mainly, I was hopeful for a major win: my own business. My own *successful* business.

It had been there all along, inside me, a creative well of potential. But it had taken an outside force to trigger my looking up from my routine existence to see it.

Momentum kept building. I called up another person who got laid off from the same company. He was more on the technical side. I asked if he wanted to work with me as a contractor and told him I'd do the sales, management, billing, planning, and the strategy if he'd do the in-platform buying and executing. He loved the idea.

So with that, I started calling companies, and several of them gave us a shot. By February 5, 2011, I had checks to deposit, and I didn't have a bank account. It was a laborious process getting a tax ID number and licensed with the state, plus filing the LLC paperwork, opening a bank account, and trying to figure out how this operation was going to work. I had clients but didn't have a business set up yet. I didn't have a website. I didn't have time to think about that. I didn't have a company name or logo. I didn't have an office. I was working from home.

I went from thinking, "Where am I going to work?" and "Who am I going to work for?" to "Oh my God, I have a business!" Which is not the way that I'd recommend most people go about it. There wasn't a lot of sleep during those first six weeks of planning and preparation. I did manage to build a Facebook page and a Twitter account in that time. It was all really fast and furious.

Yes, it was a crazy ride. Mad, stressful. But I would do it again in a heartbeat. I knew I was where I should be, and that sense of rightness bolstered me. In those first few months, I started with nothing but what was in my savings account, what we had built up as our emergency fund, my computer, and car. I was billing and generating revenue, but I didn't take a paycheck. I put it all back into the business. I wondered how I was going to bring in new business and how I was going to land clients. I had to figure out how to travel and meet with people without getting paid to do so while staying present for my family.

Putting together promotional pieces was another challenge. I did many corny things that first year, but they were effective because potential clients sensed my sincerity and ambition. On May Day, I took little flowerpots and put packets of seeds in them, along with cute fake flowers. I added cards that said, "Your business will bloom with us," or "Watch your business grow with us." For the Fourth of July, I bought cases and cases of snaps, those fun little fireworks you throw on the sidewalk to hear them pop and see them spark. I would deliver a case to a prospective client with a message taped on top of it: "Digital marketing is a snap with KeyMedia."

I'd drive all over the place, as far away as Fargo and Rapid City; Omaha and Des Moines. I'd go anywhere I could get a meeting. To save hotel costs and to make sure I wasn't gone too long from the family, I would turn around and drive home right after the meeting.

Then I'd get up at five o'clock in the morning and start my day all over again. I was super structured. I'd go work out at the gym, and then I'd come back and shower. After that, I'd get the kids up and ready for school and out the door. The first half of the workday was all business prospecting. I was dialing for dollars, calling people, trying to schedule meetings. In the afternoons, I would do all of my meetings.

I'd be home in time so that when the kids got home from school, I could help them with homework. I'd have dinner with them, put them to bed, and then process any work that I had left to finish after they went to bed.

I was working overtime to make my business successful so that ultimately I could be present with my family more. I didn't sleep a lot. I was super dedicated, because I was desperate to achieve that magic balance between career and homelife. But while I was keeping a hectic pace the first year, I was also gradually learning something mind-blowing about the prevailing wisdom the world throws at us about balancing our careers and homelife.

I had to go through more life experiences before my own personal philosophy about work-life balance emerged.

So at home I went from hearing Cole say, "I know you can't come to my games because work is more important," to "Are you *ever* going back to the office, Mom? Or are you going to be here all the time?"

I felt no twinge of conscience absorbing his perspective this time around. It was a great problem to have, the fact that I was at home so much after I started my own company. By this time my kids were older, and I was discovering they needed us to be around more than when they were babies. It seems that most parents don't comprehend that fact until they have teens, and I was no exception.

I don't mean that we should hover over our teenagers and do everything for them, but they do need our presence. It was explained to me once—and I think it's the perfect metaphor—that they need us to be that houseplant in the corner of the room. They need to know that we're there, but they don't want to hear us, and they don't want us involved. Just having that caring adult presence gives them a security and a stability and a confidence to do the right thing when they're around their friends and feeling peer pressure.

So yes, more than ever I was glad I'd made the leap into starting my own company because it was really important for me to be that steady presence, the houseplant in the corner, for my kids. I missed a lot of that with Kamie, because she was already in college, but I got the chance with Cole, and I got it with Kaylee. I'm so glad, too, because it really solidified our relationships. It also provided my children a better opportunity to engage, ask questions, and be confident in who they were growing up to be.

However, not even half a year after I started the business, my zealous commitment to balancing work and homelife was put to the test. Kamie was in college, and she had the opportunity to go to Europe for the summer semester, which had always been her dream. Prior to my getting laid off on the first of January, we'd planned that I'd fly over with her, and we'd do some traveling and sightseeing for the two weeks before she started classes. After that, I'd stick around only long enough to get her settled into her dorm room. This was my child who gets very homesick, and she'd now be living thousands of miles away—temporarily, of course—only for a couple of months. But still, it was a big deal. Some parental TLC was in order.

Of course, I had no idea I'd be running my own company when I made that promise to Kamie. I struggled with the decision for about eight to ten weeks. One day I'd be positive I should stay home. We were living on our savings account, after all. I didn't think it was wise to spend money on a two-week trip to Europe and not be here in the states when I was the only employee in the business. Then the next day, I'd think, "Wait! I'm starting this business so I can be there when my kids need me!"

It was in mid-March that I finally said to myself, "This is ridiculous. I'm building my own business for my family. I'm making these changes so my kids don't come second anymore. And here I am, putting Kamie second out of fear of not making enough money."

Kamie was twenty years old. I wondered if I'd ever get an opportunity to spend two weeks with her one-on-one again. The window for that kind of interaction was closing in on me fast. If I ever wanted to do this, it had to be right then.

So I called her up and said, "We're going to make it happen. I don't know exactly what it's going to look like, but we're going to do this." Next I called a travel agent, and we put together a plan, and what do you know? We had the most amazing time in England and Ireland! We started in Liverpool because Kamie loves the Beatles, and then we went to Ireland and met practically an entire village—they came to see the Yanks when we stopped in their only pub, and we wound up staying up very late that night drinking Guinness with them—and we even spent the night in a beautiful Irish castle before heading back to her school in England. The trip was one for the storybooks. Truly priceless. A magical time.

The coolest part of it was that my daughter's boyfriend was inspired by how much fun we had. So while Kamie was still over there studying in London, he flew over and proposed to her—in Ireland—because that had become such a special place for her as a result of the trip she took with me.

So my point is that the universe rewards faith over fear. I put it out there—my faith that the money would be fine despite my fears, because I believed my commitment to family was the right one. I had to take this trip with my daughter. I trusted that my new baby, KeyMedia, would be OK.

Up until Kamie and I flew to Europe, business was consistently steady, and I was eager to jump back in and start the ball rolling again when I returned home. But I ended up catching a cold on the plane. Ugh. The timing was so bad. I was pretty sick for three or four days and running a temperature of 102°F. Somebody tried calling me. I didn't recognize the number. But I couldn't answer the phone anyway because I had almost completely lost my voice.

I listened to the voicemail message. It was a company out of Oklahoma. They were working on a contract that they needed assistance with and were wondering if I'd give them a quote for doing some digital marketing. They said they really needed some information by the next day because they were delivering a pitch. Larger companies wouldn't talk to them because they had only $10,000 for a six-week campaign.

I emailed them my response (since I couldn't speak very well). I said I'd take it. Of course, I would. I was hungry for business! Who cared that I was croaking like a frog when I talked, and my head was swimming with a fever!

We got on the phone, and I somehow managed to hold a hoarse conversation with them punctuated by the occasional coughing fit. We worked out the details. Still hot with fever, I worked late that night to get them what they needed and sent it the next morning.

Whew! I'd done it. I leaned back and sipped on some chicken broth and felt myself beginning to perk up.

But then, two whole weeks went by. I was fully recovered and back into my routine of cold calling, holding meetings, and working on existing contracts. I assumed I'd lost the Oklahoma deal, but they called, out of the blue. I got the deal, after all! Their pitch had worked, and they were super grateful.

Even better, a month later, they called *again* and said, "You took a risk on us when nobody else would. We have this other contract, but we don't know if you have the capacity to take it because it's much larger."

My heart started beating hard. "How much larger?"

It was for $75,000.

You bet I took that contract. KeyMedia was on a roll!

After that two-week trip to Europe and the Oklahoma deal, my business blew up. My phone rang off the hook. All the conversations, activities, work, proposals, and everything else that had been going on for those first five months started to click. I firmly believe it's because I stayed aligned with my core values and beliefs, which wasn't always easy to do. I chose family first. I chose love and gratitude and keeping an open heart.

I call it my Faith over Fear prayer, or mantra of sorts, because any time I find myself hesitating between pursuing a risky goal and staying safe, I say out loud: "Faith over fear." On stressful days, I often go to sleep with those words and even wake up with them in my head and heart. They always help move me forward.

Another sign my business was snowballing the first year: I was able to reward myself with a new car long before I anticipated that day would come. I didn't like the car I already had. I hated it, in fact. When I parked it at potential clients' offices, it certainly didn't signal success. And on longer trips, it wasn't comfortable.

But I didn't feel that I could take on a car payment until I could pay myself a salary. So I waited. I set a goal that the first month I made $10,000 in profit, I'd trade in my current car and buy a new one. I mean a *new* new one (I'd actually never purchased a brand-new car before). That day came in June 2011, the month after I got back from Europe. I bought a gorgeous Subaru Legacy, silver with a black leather interior. Boy, did I love that Subaru. I drove it for a long, long time, until it had 170,000 miles on it.

Another boon after the Europe trip: I had hired a girlfriend on a part-time basis to help me with accounting, because that isn't my strength. Put me with the books, and I will struggle, which means I'll have no time to go where I can best serve the business: in biz dev and marketing. In August of my first year, I was so happy when my accountant friend was able to quit her full-time job to work for me, because there was so much business rolling in at that point.

So I was doing what I envisioned I could do. Making money on my own. Building my company. And seeing my family, too. In fact, Kamie, my newly engaged daughter, came back from Europe in August and said she and her fiancé were going to have a short engagement and get married in November. I was learning my own way to cope with all plates I had spinning at one time, so I said, "OK. Let's do this."

And we did.

Which brings me back to work-life balance. When I had complete control over my career and could no longer blame an outside force for steering me away from my core values, I saw that the concept of work-life balance—ensuring that both sides of the scale exist in equilibrium—was entirely the wrong model to consider if you want to live your best life.

A better way to look at this conundrum is *blending instead of balancing*. I highly recommend you attach that to your computer screen with a sticky note: *Blend, Not Balance!* It'll save you a lot of unnecessary grief and guilt.

In a blended world, the weights/responsibilities on both sides of the scale are going to fluctuate, and we're not going to freak out about it the way we do when we strive for balance. Sure, occasionally, a miracle will happen, and the two sides of the scale will be perfectly balanced. But for most of us, that's a rarity, and in a blended world, we don't even say balance is the big goal.

Instead of always striving to equate priorities and responsibilities on both sides of the scale, in a blended world, we embrace that often

> What item, or scenario, represents balance for you in your life?
>
> Are you able to blend your responsibilities and still reach your goals?
>
> What skills will you use to make blending happen?

they'll be in flux. We don't beat ourselves up for living real lives, where stuff happens all the time that we often can't anticipate.

For instance, right now I can say the business side of what's going on in my life has a far greater weight to it and thus a much greater demand on my time than it normally does. But there have been other times, such as when my father's health was in question or when my granddaughter was in the NICU for forty-one days, when my family commitments have taken precedence over my business agenda.

I have learned to go with the flow. First of all, I talk to everyone about what's happening. Communication is key. And then I make decisions that work best for me and my values. Sometimes I hand off responsibilities to the appropriate people. I might also take on solution-oriented tasks that best fit the context of the situation, whatever it is.

I blend when I go on vacations, too. I put out an "Out of Office" message that says I'm taking time off to focus on my family because they deserve it. But I also stay committed to the business. I tell my employees and clients that if there's something urgent that comes up that can't wait until I get back to message me and put the word *Urgent* in the headline. I will respond. But if they don't put *Urgent* in the headline, I'm not going to respond until I return.

In all the years I've been doing this, I've never had somebody send me an urgent message. They respect the fact that my family time is gold. And I do the same thing for my employees if they're on vacation. I say, don't take your computer. Or your phone. Don't check in. Don't read messages. And if something is critical that I simply can't figure out without your input—which would be extremely rare—I will shoot you a text message.

Which also doesn't happen. I want my employees to disconnect, recharge, reenergize, and focus on their families when they're not at work. Because I know when they come back, they'll be better for it.

Blending. It's an admission that each of us has unique priorities and a unique life circumstance, and that's OK. At KeyMedia, we don't do cookie-cutter balancing acts. It's futile to try, and we're smarter and more creative than that. We can handle each situation in context, and it's because our core mission is to do excellent work using the talents of employees who feel individually supported.

## "You Betcha"s

1. You betcha creative, personalized marketing impresses clients. They sense your ambition and sincerity.

2. You betcha staying aligned with your core values always pays off. You might not see results immediately, but you will eventually.

3. You betcha blending makes a lot more sense than balancing. Real life involves a lot of give-and-take between priorities at work and at home.

# Staying on Track with Success

*Fall down seven times, stand up eight.*

**—JAPANESE PROVERB**

I'd been in business for myself for three years. I grew out of my home office almost immediately and started renting office space. But it seemed like every year we were changing our address to find a larger place to accommodate our growth. At that time in the real estate market, a mortgage payment was less than a lease payment. So I began thinking about buying a commercial property. But how big a building did I want?

At that point, I realized that I needed to decide whether I was comfortable keeping the status quo—maintaining the company at its current size and not growing, which meant keeping a cozy-sized staff and a decent but more select number of clients—or did I want to take steps to grow the business big-time?

Like, go-for-the-brass-ring big?

Because, life. We each have only one, right? And did I really want to die someday with a list of regrets clenched in my fist? My parents and grandparents didn't bring me up to let fear rule me. My Higher Power had my back, too. I knew this.

But I'm only human. Of course, as with any risk, my brain, hard-wired for survival, was shooting out fear messages: *Protect yourself. Be grateful for what you already have. Don't be foolish. Don't be greedy. Use your common sense and stick with the tried-and-true.*

And I had to wonder, what if I failed? Who else would I bring down with me? A lot of people. That was no small matter to consider.

Yet because the stakes were so high, I needed to step outside my panicky thoughts—which were also valid worries—and stay calm so I could search for the best answer. Psychologists agree that the way to face our anxieties with composure is to acknowledge and talk back to those primitive fear messages that come from our limbic brain. Tens upon thousands of years ago, it served a great purpose, to let us know when saber-toothed tigers were nearby, or snakes, or raptors. And it still helps us. Its quick warning system has come to my aid many a time—like when I'm burning my hand on my oven rack at home or when I'm about to step out into traffic and pull myself back when a cyclist whizzes by in the bike lane. But danger has gotten much more theoretical since cavemen and dinosaurs roamed the earth, so these days we need to assess most threats using higher-level thinking. I've told you before that there's nothing wrong with using catchy phrases to access mental skills that help us process what's happening in our lives. So when I feel overwhelmed with red-alarm thoughts, I try to do what I call the *Limbic Limbo*. I know, I know! But remember how fun limbo was when you were a kid at the skating rink or a birthday party? Trying to get under that pole without touching it? You might have even danced under a limbo pole at an adult celebration, such as a college social event or a wedding.

Even imagining myself shimmying under and away from those primal survival thoughts my limbic brain produces allows me to shake them off—usually, because I can't help feeling kind of fun and crazy (even wily), avoiding the fearful musings symbolically hanging over me.

A less-rigid, anxious mindset—a loose, more playful one—enables me to access the more sophisticated parts of my brain to analyze stressful situations deeper.

So anyway, back to my big question—should I or should I not grow the business?—I decided, after a lot of calm thought, that if expanding the business didn't work out, I had my current business model to rely on. It worked well. We wouldn't be *destroyed*, as my limbic brain feared. We could regroup and continue the status quo.

Having mentally danced myself through the Limbic Limbo—take that, you panicky thoughts!—I was also so much more able to access hope and positivity. Gosh, what if I succeeded and the business flourished? Who could benefit from my success? A lot of people, for sure. Definitely even more than I had working for me now. I'd bring on new employees. And I'd be able to help more clients. All of that would be such a blessing.

Some of my employees especially enjoyed our smaller work environment and didn't want to expand. I didn't like to worry them about projecting a bigger vision. But it was there, in my head, calmly and prayerfully considered. My company was already helping so many people—clients, employees, and myself, along with my kids, my extended family, and my community. I had to trust that God put the idea in my heart, and I would assure any doubters in the company that together we could make growth work for us.

At the end of the day, for me a barometer for good decision-making is whether I can sleep well at night. Do I feel good about what I do each day at work with the information I have available to me? Do I make calls authentic to my values and beliefs? If circumstances were to change and I'm required to change course, do I have the resources to keep my business healthy?

For many months, before this office building came up on the market, I woke up hungry to dig deeper into the digital marketing industry, and I saw our company's great potential to do so. After having done a lot of reflection and review, I made a conscious decision that we were going to take the leap. We were going to bring in more people and really lean into the opportunities that were there instead of backing away from them.

So in 2014, I bought a commercial property, a major milestone for me and the KeyMedia team. It was a leap of faith, to be sure. But I trusted in my values. If I kept them at the forefront of all my decisions, KeyMedia would grow and prosper.

The initial plan was that the company would occupy two-thirds of our office building, and we were going to lease out one-third of it. This necessitated major construction. I remember taking quiet time to walk through the building one day and looking at the studs that were up. Nothing was sheetrocked yet. I was meditating on the space, thinking about everything going on. At that time, we had a couple of really large contracts we were bidding on that we were fairly confident we'd get. If we did, we'd need to hire more people. It hit me then: we'd need that extra one-third of the building space when those contracts materialized.

But the blueprints were drawn intentionally to separate that space from KeyMedia's portion of the floorplan. The architect had put in a small hallway and a door so the two spaces wouldn't flow. They'd be separate.

It was then, in the empty building, that I felt a surety flood my heart. KeyMedia was meant to grow. I was going all in. There would be no doorway or hall closing off that other third of the space to rent it out. At my behest, the contractors made the changes. We widened the hallway and removed that door. Moved a wall. It didn't seem separated anymore. Every room would be used by the KeyMedia family.

So what happened next? The good news is that we got into the building in April 2015. That was cause for huge celebration. The other good news is that we hired more people. Hurrah! The space was bustling with new energy.

But there was some bad news. Very bad news. We found out in June 2015 that we didn't get those big contracts I was almost positive we'd secure, and we needed that money to cushion the transition between the old status quo and our new growth. I learned the hard way, then and there, that more people go bankrupt in growth than they do in a recession.

Which makes pursuing growth a scary proposition, I know. But I assure you, risk-taking done right can pay off. Hopefully, you can learn from my mistakes.

Before we get to lessons learned, let's finish hearing about the miserable time I was having.

Have you ever felt tiny and weak in contrast to an opposing powerful force?

Did you access your values to take this force on?

If so, what values did you find within to aid you?

Were you successful?

How could we pay our bills? First, I went through all my family's cash reserves. I cashed out my life insurance. And then, I did something I hope to never, ever in my life do again: I laid off people. It pains me to even think about that.

In August of that year, after rowing upstream all spring and summer, I pulled the remaining team together and had a powwow with them. I said, "If we're going to survive this, we have to do something different. We need to get super aggressive, and we need to do it today. We have two weeks to put together a plan as to what we're going to do to turn things around and bring in new business. Everybody in the company is responsible for that, because everybody in the company will be out of a job if we don't do it."

And we did. We put together a plan, and we acted on it. By December 2015, we had signed $2 million in contracts! One started that month. The other started in January 2016. So I thought, "OK, this is good. Now we need to hire people back to do the work."

And that was when we really hit the wall. I'd been spinning lots of plates trying to keep cash flow going. But it was gone. All of it. The company was completely out of cash. As a result, we cut everything we could. There were no frills, no beer in the refrigerator. We still had free coffee, though. Always free coffee. *Free Coffee = Hope.* I should actually cross-stitch that and put it above the coffee station! Everyone needs hope. And if you can give people one small comfort that says, "I care about you; you matter," they might gain a tad more strength and inspiration to get them through the day.

By about February 2016, the company running on fumes, my operations manager, who was my first employee, and I agreed the situation was dire. Every week we prayed a check from those two big contracts would come in so payroll would clear the bank.

I also started going to banks to apply for loans to get us over the hump. Nobody would give us one, not even my own bank. They said 2015 was a little rocky for me. I lost money, so they couldn't justify it. Of course, it was the only year in business that I'd ever lost money! I told them I'd need $100,000 to see me through, and I'd pay it back ASAP. It wasn't like I was asking for $2 million. And I had a million dollars in revenue to back up my promise—one of those big contracts was a guaranteed government one.

They still refused.

For a while I'd had a business coach, but I'd let him go because of the loss of revenue in 2015. I realized I really needed an advisor, somebody to guide me through this emergency, and so I started looking around. Where could I go? Whom could I trust? Who was going to be able to help guide us through this desperate cycle we were in?

Through research I discovered Vistage, a CEO network with local chapters you can join. But to join is difficult because you have to fill out an application processed in California, and then you have to be interviewed by an executive coach. After that, you have to go to one of their meetings and be interviewed by all the members. Then you leave, and they vote on whether or not they want you in their chapter.

Those were a lot of hoops to jump through.

Most of the executives in Vistage come from large companies. I was definitely out of my league. But undeterred, I reached out and discovered a local group in Sioux Falls. In March 2016, I filled out the application and interviewed with the coach. I went to the first meeting to meet the other members and have a crucial conversation that would determine whether they'd vote me in or not.

And so I was in a room with very successful CEOs, all men except for one other woman. They owned companies that had hundreds of employees, spanning ten different states. Their businesses could claim $50 million to $200 million in revenue. And here I was with $3.2 million in revenue. Sheesh. It was easy to be intimidated, especially when these titans of industry around the conference table asked me point-blank: "Why do you want to be in this chapter? What are you looking for?"

I appreciated their straight talk. After all, joining Vistage was a big investment for a small company. I needed to be aware that I was possibly biting off more than I could chew in seeking membership.

For the large company CEOs, the price to join was not a hardship, but for a little entrepreneur like me in financial crisis, it was a substantial financial outlay.

I sensed their extreme skepticism and knew I had to impress them with my determination. But how to impress them when my business was in a bad way and I had no idea how to save it?

Luckily, I remembered what my parents and grandparents said: There is dignity in working your hardest, no matter the outcome. Sure, I was in trouble, but I had nothing to be ashamed of. I'd made my business decisions based on the information I had at the time. I could hold my head high.

## THOUGHTSHOT

Think about those words of wisdom from my family: "There is dignity in working your hardest, no matter the outcome."

*Can you share an example of when you worked your hardest— and you still fell short of your goal? What did you do next? Did you get help? If so, who helped you? Did you approach them, or did they come to you? What did you learn?*

I decided that the only way to make a good impression on this extraordinary group was to be honest. They would see, at the very least, that I had integrity.

"If I don't join," I said, "I'm going to go bankrupt. And I don't want to go bankrupt. I want to save my business. I need to be around people who can help me save my business because right now we're in dire straits. I'll take any advice you can give me, and I'll apply it tomorrow."

I could feel the strong reaction around the table. I had surprised them with my frankness. And maybe they were touched by my humble request for help. At any rate, the atmosphere became much less intimidating. They said, "OK, lay it out on the line, Korena. Tell us what you're experiencing. We're going to help you through this."

Looking back now, I see how vulnerable I was when I entered that Vistage meeting. I went in there and confessed to total strangers, all of whom were wildly successful, that I could lose my business as soon as the next day if I didn't do something immediately. That gathering made me realize, once again, how essential it is for us to help one another if we possibly can. Life is hard. I could never have gotten where I am today without the help of other people.

By the end of the Vistage get-together, I had names and phone numbers for bank connections to contact. But the most important one was an organization called B2B CFO. It comprises accountants and chief financial officers from large organizations. Most are on their way to retirement, but they're not quite ready to leave. They become consultants, affordable consultants, for small businesses that can't afford to have a CFO.

Obviously, the benefit of having this experience and knowledge is invaluable to small organizations who want to set themselves up for financial success.

So that day I called Kurt from B2B CFO and said, "I got your name from the Vistage meeting. Would you be willing to sit down and talk with me?"

"Absolutely," he said. He answered my call for help.

Despite the seriousness of my predicament, I felt hopeful and excited. We set up a meeting for that week. He and I sat down, and I literally put all the papers in front of him and said, "I don't know what to do, but we're in crisis. We need really fast answers."

Normally, they do an evaluation and come back to you with a plan to implement. At that point, you can hire them to help you carry out the plan on an as-needed basis. It was super affordable at about a hundred dollars an hour. Usually, these accountants and CFOs make at least $300 an hour.

I said, "I don't have two weeks to wait for you to do an evaluation. I don't have it."

"OK," he said. "Let me dig into everything. I'll call you tomorrow."

Just like that, he jumped in and helped work us through a plan. He got us funding to get us past the cash flow problem. We had probably about ten to fifteen hours a month of his time for that first year. He came in and learned our business, and then he taught my team and me how to understand the financials better so that we wouldn't ever be in that position again. He helped us execute on that consistently.

But more importantly, he still consults with us. We built out a three-year plan together and put systems and processes in place that enabled us to pay more attention to things that we needed to keep an eye on that we had no idea we needed to heed before. He also gave us a plan to pay off the loan we received to get through the crisis, and we fully paid that off last year.

We're debt free again.

I'm still in Vistage. They voted me in, which was such an honor. But what really affects me emotionally—when I think about the people around that boardroom table at our first meeting—is how if I had not gone into that conversation being fully transparent, I would not be in business today. I would've lost my business that year. So I owe Vistage and its caring members so much. One way I can pay them back is to pass on my lessons learned to other entrepreneurs, both ones who approach Vistage for guidance and other entrepreneurs, like you.

Vistage's lessons continue to impact my revenue. We ended 2020 up 25 percent over 2019, and KeyMedia's success is continuing to grow.

\#

I look back now and can't believe how close I came to shutting down KeyMedia for good in 2016. It's no wonder that during that stressful time I couldn't sleep at night. It was because people relied on me for their livelihoods. They were supporting their families. I would have given away every single thing I owned before I ever told them I couldn't make payroll.

Before and during that crisis, I was making the best decisions I could based on the information I had. However—and this is the kicker—there were things I didn't know about growth that I didn't know I should know! It was a soul-crushing lesson. My limited perspective was causing my problems and preventing me from finding solutions.

So, how to fix a limited perspective? Education. Where does that come from? Wisdom from your own hard-knock experience—which we arrive at only after we already need it—and other people's knowledge, which thankfully, we can tap into before an emergency happens.

Seriously, if your business is faltering and you're seeking mentorship, you have to be honest. And you have to expose your weaknesses. I had to be both authentic and vulnerable to get the best help I could. Vistage and B2B CFO would not have worked with me, otherwise.

So many of us think that if we're the big boss, we should know what to do. But take it from me—the reality is that even CEOs of major companies can use advice and seek it out. Sadly, some businesses fail because their CEOs don't seek help or they put it off too long.

I love that mentoring groups like Vistage and B2B CFO exist and really wanted to share that with you—that you don't have to go it alone. Coaching is a win-win for everyone. People with tremendous stores of knowledge pass on their skills so that their hard-won wisdom is not lost when they retire. The whole concept of mentorship is neighborly and positive.

Receiving assistance from businesspeople who could help get my company to the next level helped me become a better CEO, coach, and team leader. And let me tell you, it's always hard for me to ask for anything. But thank goodness I did. You can, too.

Then in 2022 I took on another challenge and purchased a twenty-two-thousand-square-foot, severely neglected, commercial building. Navigating the process felt like I was hearkening all the way back to my troubles in 2015 and 2016. That was when I learned that teamwork is the difference between survival and bankruptcy, between a boom or a bust year.

Let me catch you up. Purchasing this building was a bit of a challenge for a few reasons. One, it was a total flip job. There was nothing salvageable about it except for the outside. And two, the sellers have changed some terminology on the contract. I'd already signed it, but before they signed, they changed some wording.

To make sure I had my ducks in a row, I had to look outside my own limited experience with construction and commercial real estate contracts and hire some experts. I worked with an engineer and an attorney, a real estate broker, and my banker. Lots of moving parts. We all came together as a team with a weekly conference call. Together, we walked through the contract and the construction plan to make sure my interests were identified properly and met.

Later, I met with Kurt, my B2B CFO mentor. I caught up with him over breakfast, and I told him I had been putting stuff together to buy this new building, and I wanted him to review all the numbers to make sure I wasn't missing anything. After looking through all the paperwork, he said, "I think you've got it nailed. I don't see anything that's off on this. You're good to go."

Having a cohort of trusted advisors can make all the difference! Their knowledge, insights, and experience fill the gaps that I am missing and build confidence in the ideas and plans I am generating. But, this only works when I listen and apply their advice.

Scott Bendor, a professor at the Stanford Graduate School of Business, was studying what traits comprise the best teams, and he noted that the right mix of tools and talents is essential. He said, "When everybody's swinging hammers and no one's sawing lumber, the house won't get built."

Bottom line, all my professional success goes back to my having a wonderful team. None of us can possibly know everything. Having good consultants supporting your agenda makes all the difference. When I finally woke up and realized how crucial a great team is, I focused on getting people together who have different strengths and perspectives. And boy, I'm glad I did. Together, we complement one another, and we get that metaphorical house that Bendor is talking about *built*.

## "You Betcha"s

1. You betcha being both authentic and vulnerable can gain you respect, even if you're failing at something. It might even compel the right people to assist you.

2. You betcha CEOs can't afford to pretend they know everything. Coaching is a great investment of your time and money.

3. You betcha assembling a supportive team comprising members with complementary strengths is the key to success through good times and bad.

# Embrace the Challenges That Come with Success

*No one would have crossed the ocean if he could have gotten off the ship in the storm.*
**—CHARLES KETTERING**

Achieving success doesn't mean life gets easy. No, it's hard to be in business. As you become more successful, as I have, the challenges evolve. They not only don't go away, but they also get more difficult. But trials and tribulations are part of the nature of business, so you have to learn to deal with them. If you have the right mindset, your challenges will be the making of you and your company.

## THOUGHTSHOT

My male friends and colleagues don't always recognize the additional hardships women face because of our responsibilities outside the workplace and the unique approach we bring to leading our businesses. I'm a nurturer and proud of it, at home and at work. I want to guide my children and grandchildren, and it's important to me to mentor my employees as well. I care about them. I care about our clients. I want everyone to rise.

> *Are you a nurturer? Is that a description of yourself you embrace? Or does someone else in your life come to mind first? Discuss what it means to you to be a person who cares about helping others. How is your understanding of what it means to nurture reflected in your daily life?*

I gladly work my butt off to aid and inspire people to reach their goals and dreams every day. Despite my obvious success using this approach—my company is thriving, and my employees and customers are happy—I still face discrimination in the workplace simply because of my gender.

It's well documented that female entrepreneurs have a harder time succeeding than their male counterparts. Let's hope things will change in the next generation. Right now, women spend way more time than men ensuring our homes are running well: we take on about 65 percent of domestic chores. We're spinning more plates, and we're also paid less than men for the same job. This layered bias against women is rooted in the outdated belief that we can't excel at our jobs if we're also trying to be a good spouse, parent, caregiver to aging parents, and neighbor.

I believe it all started with men believing this very thing about themselves—that they have to be all about the job, or they will fall behind their peers.

So when women dare to do both, and succeed as so many have, this hollow principle that giving over your whole identity to work is exposed for what it is: baloney.

Now it's time for men to do their part at home. COVID-19 awakened a lot of them. Men have given themselves permission to enjoy their homelife, to participate in the rearing of their children, to see themselves apart from their office persona.

COVID-19 and the way it turned everyone's world upside down is one reason I feel we have a real chance for cultural change. Homelife matters. Period. It's refreshing to see some high-profile male executives at Apple and Google fight against going back to the way things were pre-COVID-19. Some of them have quit in protest. Yay. All this helps the cause of women, who have known all along how important it is to nurture a private life apart from work.

And let's not forget that the bias against women in business over the years has come from men and women, both. Whether we're talking boorish bosses, competitive *Devil Wears Prada* workmates, or judgey types of any stripe, women have endured soul-crushing prejudices at work when all we wanted was to be able to do our jobs and not feel guilty about prioritizing our home lives, too.

I don't want any woman reading this to take negative cultural messages as a sign to give up on your dreams. Trust that things are changing. Don't let fears or imposter syndrome prevent you from launching your own business. You can do it. You've had a lot of women who've come before you. And we have to keep pushing boundaries. I love being part of the change for our daughters and granddaughters. It motivates me in a huge way to succeed beyond the naysayers' expectations. And don't forget my adage: *Blend, not balance.* I swear it's worked wonders for me. So hang in there.

And to the men reading this: Even if you don't necessarily agree with me that women have a harder time at work, I'd appreciate your sticking around to hear my viewpoint. I'm not here to vent frustration or cast blame. Seriously. My goal is to share what I've experienced, so it will become part of the ongoing dialogue about women in the American workplace. Conversations can enlighten everyone on all sides and possibly effect change for the better.

Yes, I'll bring up some disagreeable scenarios that have happened to me, personally, but only in the hope that I can help another woman who finds herself in a similar position. It might also help men think twice about how they approach their interactions with women in the workplace—certainly not make you frightened to talk but to come from a place of better understanding, with a softer approach.

Let's start with one of my stories—one of many I could tell about how I've come up against unsupportive postures regarding my place at the entrepreneurial table. A couple of years ago, South Dakota's state legislature was considering taxing advertising, and not everyone was on board. In fact, one of our lawmakers had put together a committee of media owners within the state to discuss how that tax would impact our businesses. The plan was to gather information to be able to fight the legislation.

I walked into this meeting, and with the exception of our state representative, there were fifteen men ten-plus years older than I was. Among them was a gentleman who owned a large radio group, the president of a local TV station, and the South Dakota Newspaper Association's board of directors—pillars of our state's media community. As we were getting settled in, a former boss of mine came up and slapped me on the back.

"Hey, kiddo," he said, loud enough for everyone to hear. "Why are *you* here?"

My stomach immediately clenched. I don't remember what I replied, exactly, but it was something jokey yet polite, like, "I'm here for the same reason you are."

He grinned. I smiled tightly. Inside, insecurities bubbled up. *Could I contribute? Did I have the right level of experience to have an opinion on this issue? Did I have a right to be here?* We went back and forth another minute with small talk, and then I excused myself and made a beeline—a slow, cool one—for the bathroom. I walked with my head held high.

But once I entered the sanctuary of that tiled space, empty except for me, I looked in the brightly lit mirror and gave myself a mental pep talk: *You have definitely earned the right to be here, Korena. You deserve to be sitting around that table. You have plenty to contribute.*

I felt buoyed by my own belief in myself, and honestly, it was a little crazy that it had to come to that: Coach Korena's version of a locker room speech before a big game, delivered to myself! I realize now I carried Coach Korena along with me for years. Yep, I talked myself up *to* myself. It worked, so why not? It's sad that women don't often have true mentors they can turn to for support at work—people we can open up to and be our genuine selves with. We walk our entrepreneurial path alone, many times, and that's unnecessary and should change. Until it does, you give yourself all the locker room talks you need to in the ladies' room!

> Where do you go to pull yourself together and gain a little confidence?
>
> Is it a physical space?
>
> Or a practice you rely on?
>
> Has this changed in any way over the years?

My old boss knew how much I'd accomplished since I'd moved on from his company. We lived in a small town. He was well aware that I was a serious businesswoman. Yet he did nothing to support me that day. To add insult to injury, he made sure the other men witnessed him putting me in what he thought was my place, subordinate to him and not qualified to participate in that meeting.

Ultimately, I proved him wrong that day. I did belong there. In fact, the state representative called on me several times, and my voice was heard. I wasn't discredited at all, and the rest of the meeting went well.

#

It's easy to rationalize small slights. People have bad days. They don't mean anything by it. It's simply a careless remark. A joke. Everyone should lighten up. Have a sense of humor.

But after a while, little barbs and degradations add up. If you're a woman in business, and you hear them over and over from your male colleagues, yes, they can affect your commitment to your goals if you let them. It hurts not to be taken seriously, especially when you're the most serious person in the room. At this point in our culture, female entrepreneurs have to develop a thick skin—a thicker skin than their male counterparts—to succeed. Again, there is no reason this state of affairs should continue without being challenged. It's wrong and must change.

Sadly, I have another personal example of bias against women in the workplace: On January 1, 2011, when I got laid off at that digital start-up, the one that shut down and led me to the life-changing decision to start my own business, my former boss passed a contract to me that he'd signed months before to host an internet café at a conference in mid-January. By the time the conference rolled around, I'd decided to start my new company, so in effect, KeyMedia wound up hosting the café. Super excited, I let the conference-goers know I was in business for myself from home. These were people I trusted. I'd been on boards with or worked with many of them. I thought of them as friends who'd support me. Who'd celebrate with me.

But overwhelmingly from the older men, I heard, *Yeah, right. You're not going to work from home. You just want to stay in your pajamas and hang out with your kids. This isn't going to work, Korena. Forget it.*

Back then, working from home was not a popular trend. As for a woman working from home? Those guys were sure I'd be running a sham operation. I'd be too tethered to my domestic responsibilities—and maybe bonbons and soap operas?—to provide legitimate digital marketing services, much less make any money doing so.

I was so disappointed at their condescending response, but I didn't let them get me down. I merely replied, "You can watch me make it happen. Failure is not an option for me." And let them go on their merry way. They'd regret their words, soon enough, I knew.

Even so, their scorn rattled me, and I had to wonder what made it OK for my male colleagues to behave so poorly. The culture was to blame, of course. We say what we can get away with. I decided then and there that I could at least work on changing the local zeitgeist. I would become so successful, next time those guys held a bro-fest, they'd think, "As long as Korena Keys is in business, we don't have a leg to stand on with these 'women in the workplace' jokes."

A girl can dream, right?

Since then, I've seen these smarty pants many a time and taken great delight in having proven them wrong. *Incredibly* wrong. I can chuckle now thinking about it. The joke was most definitely on them, but I also hope they learned something important from watching me prosper: *Girl power. It's a real thing. Deal with it.*

Speaking of amusing, a few years later, when KeyMedia was well-established and very successful, I had to tell a guy who interviewed for a job with us that he wasn't the right fit. I explained as nicely as possible—because it's never easy to hear you've been rejected—that my employees have a say in who we'll hire as they'll be the ones working with that person, and unfortunately, he'd been voted down. At that point in our chat, the former candidate for a job advised me not to listen to my employees. He explained—or mansplained, if we're going to use a new word from *Webster's*—that I was the person in charge. Therefore, I should be the sole arbiter of who gets hired.

"Hmm. Thank you for telling me how to run my company," I thought. At the door I told him that as CEO of the company, I value employee input when it comes to hiring people and wished him well. I found out later he'd messaged all the men who worked for me and asked them to help set me straight. Sheesh.

I don't want to give the impression that only men have had trouble with my entrepreneurial aspirations. I've dealt with women, too, who simply can't accept that the buck stops with me, that I ultimately hold the reins at KeyMedia. Even a female employee once challenged me on this. We weren't giving her everything she wanted, apparently, and so she came to me to chat about her needs, which I was happy to do. But what it turned out to be, actually, was an ultimatum. She wasn't happy, so it was me or her, she said. One of us had to go.

"You mean leave the company?" I asked.

"Yes." She tossed her head and waited.

I looked behind me at the wall and then back at her. "Um, I guess it'll have to be you. My name is on the checks you cash." She didn't last long.

I know it sounds crazy that she thought I was a figurehead and there was someone else actually running the place—like Oz behind his curtain in *The Wizard of Oz*. But she did. It was beyond her grasp that her female employer—who happened to be empathetic and generous—could possibly be the big boss, too. It was sad, really. Obviously, we need more female role models at work so that young girls grow up believing that becoming a successful entrepreneur is possible for them.

I also don't want to suggest that the skeptics in my life have been only professional colleagues, acquaintances, or strangers I've crossed paths with at work. Nope. My own father had issues with my business goals, as did the man I was married to when I started KeyMedia.

My dad doubted me for a long time. It was hard because there's no question he loves me and wants me to be successful. But several times he'd asked me as I struggled to get my company off the ground, "Are you sure you're doing the right thing? You're going to look back at this time and regret it." He was referring to my time away from the kids.

My father had a lot of remorse about working and traveling so much when all his kids were home. He hadn't been as involved with us growing up as he'd really wanted to be. And he didn't want me to make those same mistakes.

I understood that. So I wasn't mad at him for sharing his concerns. But, of course, I wasn't going to neglect my children. I reminded Dad that my intention when I started my business wasn't to have a huge company. It was to be able to do my part in supporting my family, not so we could be wealthy and drive brand-new cars but so we could live comfortably while giving me the flexibility to be there for my kids when they needed me. I assured Dad that I wanted to make sure my children knew they were important, my number one priority.

I explained my vision to my dad on many occasions, but he didn't quite grasp it. My mom was also struggling to understand what I was doing and why. It likely didn't help that they truly did not understand the business services or what I actually worked on every day.

It took a long time, probably five years, for my parents truly to comprehend why I was doing what I was doing. Back in 2016, when I'd bought my first office building, remodeled it, and moved in, KeyMedia had an open house to celebrate. I think that was the light bulb moment for Mom and Dad. They walked in, saw the gorgeous office space and all the people involved—excited employees and clients—and figured out that, oh, this isn't just a little project on the side for me. And I'm not neglecting my family. I was showing my children they could create something wonderful from sheer hard work and persistence.

That day Dad said he was really proud of me. I'd chased my dream and caught it. Both my parents said they could see how well things were going and that my business life was impacting my children in a positive way.

For me, that was a major success moment.

I've talked about some of the hardships I've experienced as a business-woman. But I haven't touched yet on the most painful challenge I've been through on my road to success. This pushback came from my now ex-husband.

Ladies, as many of you have shared with me over the years, when our spouses or partners work against us and our dreams, it's devastating. We understand why our children might, right? They're young. They need reassurance. When it's our parents, we know they're protective and simply don't want us to get hurt. Their concern can extend to their grandkids, too.

But when it's our spouses or partners bringing us down—the people who are supposed to support our dreams and respect us for trying to achieve them—there truly is no more depleting kind of energy. It's like going up the down escalator 24-7, walking and walking, striving to reach the top, skipping steps, even. But a mate's disparaging remarks, unhelpful attitudes, and sometimes passive-aggressive actions are the descending staircase pushing us back down, keeping us from rising.

It's exhausting, and often, it can mean the end of a relationship. Mine ended, for sure, although I tried for years to make it work. My husband had been urging me to make money, but when I started my company, he was against it. He didn't believe it would work. He thought I was wasting my time and the household's slim resources.

It only got worse. When I began to gain major traction at KeyMedia, our relationship floundered. "You run the house, you take care of the kids, you make more money than I do," he used to say. "Where do I fit into this picture?"

I desperately wanted our marriage to work, so I tried to get him involved in the business. I made him 40 percent owner of the LLC I put together to handle the purchase of our company's real estate. I gifted him that percentage because I wanted him to feel important to me as his wife and to the company, which I was building for us and our children. I wished he could appreciate that, but instead he resented me.

When things got really bad, we moved into a bigger house, a nicer neighborhood, to get a fresh start. But it wasn't enough for him. Nothing ever seemed to be enough. I didn't realize at the time, but he'd been romantically involved with other people for years.

No wonder I was getting nowhere solving our marital problems!

At any rate, in September 2017, we divorced. I wanted it to be amicable, so we didn't use attorneys. We split everything except my business. We sold the house, halved the proceeds, did the same with what was in our savings, and paid off the debt that we had, which wasn't a lot at the time. He kept his retirement, and I kept mine—which was really the business. I didn't have a huge 401(k) then because throughout the marriage we'd kept cashing it out whenever we needed money.

We got through that painful process, but it wasn't long before I realized it was going to be really hard to have my ex-husband still own part of the LLC I established that KeyMedia rents from, especially as I was building a lot of equity in that business. I didn't want to gift him a portion of my hard work over the next ten, fifteen, or even twenty years. So I started the proceedings to buy him out.

That got really ugly. He wanted a lot more money than what the LLC was worth at the time. We fought more about that than we did about the entire rest of the divorce proceedings. He had no legitimate reason to want that 40 percent except that he was banking on it for his retirement plan. He felt it was unfair that I was trying to take it away from him.

But again, why should I work hard to give him some of my earnings in perpetuity? I kicked myself for my naivete in not protecting my business interests better. But hindsight is twenty-twenty. I'd been anxious to keep our family unit intact. That's why I risked giving him that equity. I was counting on us staying husband and wife.

So I decided to forgive myself. There are worse failures. I needed to focus on the present and my future. I needed to move on.

Actually, it didn't really matter how either of us felt about the matter. My bank wouldn't allow me to buy my ex-husband out. They said we needed somebody else with a higher credit rating than I had to purchase his shares. Not only that, when I'd earlier contacted the bank to say, "I got divorced, and we need to take my ex's name and access off of these business accounts," they wouldn't cooperate.

A week after I told my bank about the divorce, suddenly my account went into a review. I had to jump through hoops to prove to them that I was financially stable and that I was not relying on my ex-husband for alimony. It was a ridiculous three-month ordeal. I was required to provide copies of the divorce papers and sign affidavits that I wasn't getting alimony or paying him alimony.

I have not talked to a single man getting a divorce who's had a similar experience. Ladies, this is a warning to you—choose your bank carefully.

At the time I was making triple what my ex was making. All the bank had to do was look at our tax returns. But they hemmed and hawed. They also wouldn't loan me the money to buy him out. (If I'd paid him a fair price for his 40 percent, I wouldn't have had to take out a loan. But no. I settled on an exorbitant sum to be able to close that book, so I needed a loan to do it.)

The shoddy treatment by this bank continued. They wouldn't even allow me to take my ex-husband off the mortgage or the deeds because they felt I was not financially stable and secure as a single person.

This was a regional bank I'd been with for *five years*. It wasn't like they didn't know me. They also knew my difficult situation. I don't know why they turned on me like that, but it was challenging and frustrating. Again, they insisted I identify another business partner with a higher credit rating, although my credit rating wasn't bad. It was something like 780. We never paid a bill late. Never missed a mortgage payment.

Yet, that was what the bank demanded. So I chose my father, who was retired. He said he would absolutely become my partner; God bless him. He came in at 25 percent of the business, and I was able to remove my ex's share entirely.

Whew!

The irony of it all was that the bank was essentially saying, here's a retired guy living on his retirement fund and a fixed income, and it's OK for him to secure the loan but not his daughter, who owns a thriving business. There were so many things wrong about the situation. I never would have guessed in a million years that I'd have gone through an intense audit with them because I got divorced. Of course, they adamantly denied the reason why, because I could have sued them for discrimination. They claimed it was entirely random—really? A week after I told them I was officially divorced!

I knew and they knew that the audit had everything to do with the fact that I was a businesswoman on my own, and my status didn't match their "ideal client" profile.

After the dust had settled, you betcha I switched banks. And that's not easy when you have a business. But it was worth the hassle. My current banker says, "Eh, you're good. We've got you. You just tell us what you're going to do. Shop with confidence. Find what you need. We've got you covered."

And the thing is, they're both similar-sized banks. But the difference in the relationship and the trust and support has been night and day.

My best advice for you, whatever your gender or marital status, is to find a commercial banker who's looking to build a partnership with you and not just provide a service for you. Ask good questions. Are they willing to give you referrals to your business, based on all their connections and the other businesses they work with? Because if they're willing to do that, then they're going to support you and back you in other areas. It's important to get to know them and understand the requirements they have.

Other questions to ask: How easy is it to get credit? How much are they going to offer you? And even if you can't get the credit you think you want right now, are they willing to work with you to figure out how to get you to a point to where you can get it?

Remember, relationship. Partnership. That's what you want in your bank. My current banker, at least once a month, will shoot me a text message and ask, "How is everything going? Is there anything I can do for you?" It's a completely different relationship. In fact, he came to my house to sign papers one day. I was working from home, and I had a short window between meetings. He was working from home because of COVID-19, and we needed to get some papers signed. He literally drove to my house with his kids in his car. And we signed the papers on the hood of his car in my driveway.

Now that's what I call a great relationship with a banker. It makes me feel hope—hope that times are changing, and women in the workplace are garnering the respect and admiration they deserve.

Some battles end abruptly, and others take a long time to conclude. Workplace bias against women continues all over the world. But it's better than it used to be. Progress is being made. I'm doing my part to help shift attitudes in my family, at work, and in my community, and I feel good about that. But there is always more to be done, so let's not get complacent. Let's mentor our female entrepreneurs and help our male colleagues appreciate the joys that come with being fully present at home.

The battles with my ex have never really ended. But I learned long ago that I had to forgive him and move on. I can't be whole if I hold onto bitterness and anger. I told you that I'm a nurturer, at home and at work, and I'm not going to let him change that about me.

More than ever, I look up and rely on God to keep me grounded. It's funny, but I like talking to God in the shower. I'd call it my *Higher Power Shower Hour*, but I'm only in there about ten minutes! That's all right, though. God appreciates every moment we can give Him. So really, I just call it my Me-Time with God. He understands. He doesn't need frills and catchy phrases from us. He only wants our hearts.

I'll admit that many a time, I have felt so tired, sad, or worried that I've had no sense of God's presence. It's at those moments where

I'll simply hold open a space and say, "God, I can't feel you. But I know you never abandon me."

And He never has. I'm getting married again to a wonderful man. My fiancé is extremely supportive of everything I do. He knows how much I love my kids and grandkids. He gets that KeyMedia is my baby, as well, and that I love being able to help my employees and clients reach their goals.

I feel blessed.

I hope you trust that even when times are tough and you feel alone, if you believe in yourself and your Higher Power, things *will* get better. I wish that peace for you, the kind that sustains you in the middle of the storms that enter everyday life.

## "You Betcha"s

1. You betcha the naysayers will try to shake your confidence. But remember it's often because they are playing by stale rules. So feel sorry for them and show them how success is done with your unique brand of courage and vision!

2. You betcha who you bank with matters. Ask the right questions before you sign on because it's not easy to switch. You and your banker should have a real relationship.

3. You betcha some spouses or partners can resent your success. If this happens to you, you have my sympathy. Everyone has to work this issue out their own way. But I hope it helps you to know that I'm in a relationship now with a man who loves me for who I am, and he is proud of what I do.

# Making a Difference in Your Corner of the World

*We make a living by what we get,*
*but we make a life by what we give.*
**—WINSTON CHURCHILL**

W e all want our lives to mean something. Since I was a little girl, I felt drawn to the idea that we are here for a reason: to make good use of our time and talents to better ourselves and share our gifts with others. My parents and grandparents instilled that principle in me by example. They worked hard and led simple, good lives. Their quietly heroic stories will largely remain within our family, but they are giants in my heart, embodying the best of what humanity has to offer. I am proud to embrace their values and pass them down to my children.

Every one of us can make a difference in our corner of the world. And helping one person matters just as much as helping a hundred, or a thousand, or a million. You might ask yourself, how can this be? Aren't those rare few people in a position to make a worldwide, positive impact somehow better than the rest of us? And shouldn't we aspire to have as wide an influence as they do?

The answer to both questions is no. You were meant to be who you are. I was meant to be who I am. Some of us are roses. Others of us are daisies. And still others are dandelions, which have their own beauty if we allow ourselves to see it. My point is that we are all precious creations growing in the same garden. Each of us has a unique perspective—our own special gifts, our own Flower Power, I like to call it—to bring to the table. If we waste time comparing ourselves to others—those passions and talents we have to offer the world—the chance to blossom into our best selves could very well be lost.

So love yourself where you are, and don't hesitate to get to work impacting your corner of the world in a positive way, however imperfect you believe you, your timing, and your circumstances are. As the old saying goes, "Bloom where you are planted." Maybe you'll hug your child a little harder this morning. Or you'll support someone on Instagram by liking their post about their hobby. Or you'll go to work today and really listen to what other people have to say instead of putting yourself on autopilot so you can get through the day and just get back home.

We often assume our neighbor, boss, or sister will make the much-needed effort to help out where needed. We shut our hearts and our doors and think it doesn't matter. Who is keeping an eye on what we choose to do or *not* to do?

I'm here to remind you that we can't hide, although many of us retreat, if we can, to our own private spaces. I'd like you to look up, this time to our amazing earth, which is transporting us through a vast, mysterious universe while we tiny beings upon it—with our beating hearts and vulnerable bodies—are buckled down for the ride by the invisible force of gravity. We take our precarious existence so much for granted, don't we? But every moment we're alive is a miracle, and one that we did not earn. We've been gifted this existence. It's good to remember that.

Now, you've seen sidebars throughout these chapters with some questions that I think are important for you to consider. But when it comes to the idea of our very existence, of how we spend our time on this earth, I felt it was time to break from here so we can ask ourselves some truly revelatory questions:

- How do you feel physically when you reach out and help other people? How does it feel emotionally? Do you do it very often?

- Establishing healthy boundaries is a big topic of conversation these days. Are some walls necessary? If so, what are they? Do some walls harm more than help? What are they? As women (with many of us being nurturers), how can we manage being overrun sometimes with demands on our time and energy?

- How do you snap out of it when you feel you don't care about anyone else's problems but your own? What do you tell yourself when you feel that "survivors" need to steamroll anything in your way?

- Finally, do you ever feel alone? If so, name a few people, or even one, you can honestly reach out to for support. If you don't have any support, please be brave and seek it. Start with your neighbors if you're friendly with them, your place of worship if you go, and, of course, your place of business—talk to your boss, your HR manager, a colleague. And you can always ask a doctor to lead you to someone who can support you. But don't give up. People want to be there for you.

So let's make the most of our time here. Let's be grateful for the chances we have to give back. What I do affects you, and what you do impacts me. It defies simple explanation, but somehow our choices leave their mark. Through the complex chain of human interaction, we touch the lives of everyone else on this spinning, blue-and-green orb we call home.

## THOUGHTSHOT

One big way I feel called to make a positive difference in the world is to help create a framework of support between women, so this chapter is dedicated to working women everywhere, especially those who have been marginalized and are struggling to hold on to their dreams.

*Does this mission resonate with you? If so, what can you do where you are to help connect women, especially entrepreneurial women, and raise them up?*

*Take a look around your corner of the world. What else needs doing that your heart clamors to help with? How can you start? Are you already involved? If so, what are you doing? Have you made any progress? Remember, taking one step forward is better than doing nothing at all.*

I would love men to read what I have to say, too, to understand more about our struggles and to be inspired to advocate for women they care about. But why does helping other women feel like a special mission for me? It's because I've been there. I know what it feels like to struggle alone against opposing forces. As I've mentioned before, it's all too common that women don't find the encouragement we need to thrive in the business world. We've long worked around patriarchal biases still at play in our culture, but sadly, sometimes negativity from other women accounts for the dearth of support.

I hate to say it, but sabotage within the sisterhood is real and can be intentional. It's happened to me. But I'm self-aware enough to understand that some of that negativity might come from unconscious insecurities. I've had them my whole life and have had to battle to keep them at bay. It's only human to want to fight for what you want, and the desire to succeed in the marketplace and become a leader in our communities has been tamped down in women for far too long.

But thanks to the brave, resourceful women who came before us and laid a path forward, the next several generations are now openly determined to be successful, and that's a great thing! I'm happy to say that amazing opportunities for women open up every day, thanks to our own courage and vision.

We can still do better. Raise your hand if you're a woman who's had to be aggressive around your male counterparts to get ahead. I count myself as one. For many women, being aggressive to reach our goals is not our intuitive choice. We prefer to connect, to network, to stay positive with other people. But sometimes we find ourselves steamrolling other women who stand in our way instead of collaborating and supporting one another. Common wisdom tells us we have to. But no. We don't. We need to talk back to the culture that says aggression equals success.

Don't get me wrong. In my experience it's probably four or five men to every woman who turns cutthroat. I'll also grant that for a lot of men, their hostility stems from insecurities, too, or unconscious bias. So it's complicated.

But what we women should do is talk to one another about how we do business and how we can improve the way we interact in the marketplace. As we continue to make strides in the workforce, we have the opportunity to effect change for the better. We prefer to work in a positive setting. We don't want to sacrifice compassion and integrity to achieve success. And I'm finding out that most of the men I've worked with want the same. They've just been too trapped by the bro culture to admit it.

Hey, we women have a chance to save them. Wouldn't that be great?

I'm not spouting empty, feel-good words here. I've been running a company for a long time. I've found the majority of people I encounter in business—when I lead with my core values as the nurturer I am—jump at the opportunity to do the right thing, to be the hero, to support, to show compassion and understanding. And the more they do, the more they begin to recognize that they can move forward and be successful being a nice person.

In fact, all of us can be *more* successful when we aren't afraid to lead with our hearts, as most women I know already do. It's amazing to see the transformation in my colleagues who've never reached out to work with others because they distrust other people's motives. But when we take the time to truly see, appreciate, and encourage one another, it's like a light turns on in our souls. We recognize that every one of us has dreams for ourselves and our families. We can honor that commitment we all share by maintaining our integrity and compassion for others in the marketplace. Our mutual awareness builds bridges between us as we discover that we can reach our goals working together far faster than when we stay in our own lane.

As working women aligned with our core values, we can spread this hopeful message far and wide and show that it pays off with genuine, positive results.

Of course, the quickest way to change a culture is to speak through the voice of the majority. Alas, women are far from dominating the workplace. On the bright side, however, it's good to have big goals. They give our lives purpose. I like to envision our daughters and granddaughters thanking us someday for doing our part to change the numbers.

Let's look at them briefly without flinching, much as we might want to. The first woman CEO of a Fortune 500 company was selected in 1972, the late Katharine Graham of the *Washington Post*. Yay, Katharine! She is quite the role model. But as recently as 1995, there were no females on the Fortune 500 CEO list. Ouch.

Wait—it gets a little better. As of 2020, guess what percentage of Fortune 500 companies had a female CEO? I won't leave you to wonder. That was the year it was the highest it's ever been, at 7.4 percent. At that time, a total of thirty-seven women headed major firms.

A standing O for those amazing women!

But yes, we still have a lot of work to do. I'm up for the challenge, and I hope you are, too. Let's talk about how to build out your support network, professionally and personally. And we have to touch base with the working mothers among us because they have their own unique challenges.

One national group working to change the imbalance in those statistics we just covered is eWomenNetwork. They're a fantastic network of women with local chapters and national conferences. They hold online events and generate business directories. I wish I could still be an active member—I was for several years—but I have so much going on now; I've had to move on. However, I highly recommend it for any female entrepreneur who wants support as she grows her business.

I also recommend joining whatever groups you can find specific to the industry you're working in, and if you're a woman, see if there is a subset group within that which focuses on the needs of female members. For instance, I'm a member of the Agency Management Institute, an organization that brings agency owners across the country together to try to help one another be successful. But within that larger framework, we've created a cohort of women that meets virtually once every eight weeks to share challenges we're facing. It's been so helpful.

In my Vistage group, too, we have a group dedicated only to women's issues. We do a women-only conference every year as well as different events throughout the year for the women CEOs in the organization. It's such a comfort to feel support at that level. It's great to be there, but it can get lonely at the top, believe me.

And then, there's NWBOC, the National Women Business Owners Corporation. It helps minority businesses get federal contracts by certifying women-owned businesses. They hold conferences and training throughout the year that you can participate in as well.

Professional organizations, especially those that cater specifically to the needs of women, can really bolster female entrepreneurs in the workplace. They have helped me immeasurably. But there is more to creating opportunities for yourself. If you want to become the first female CEO of any company, or your own, it's not an easy journey. It's attainable, but it's hard. Sacrifices must be made along the way. Commitment to the goal is imperative. As I've said before, we really need advocates to help us get there.

Let's talk about having specific individuals in your life who support your entrepreneurial dreams and understand what the journey is. I have some really great friends, but there are some I can't talk to about the business because they don't understand my experience. Thankfully, I have two close girlfriends who do get it, and they are lifesavers. I didn't meet them purely by accident, either. It was because

I was networking, hoping to connect with like-minded women. We crossed paths, and—boom—we were a great match.

One of the women I met through a mutual friend, who was doing some training and had invited both of us independently to his kickoff event. At the end of it, she came up to me and said, "I've heard your name around, but we've never actually met. And I just wanted to introduce myself and say hi." We chatted for three minutes, and that was it. But the next day, I felt like I really needed to follow up with that person. So I looked her up and sent her an email that said, "I feel like we need to have lunch. Can we? Do you have time?"

Long story short, it took us a month to get together for lunch, but it ended up lasting two and a half hours. There was an instant connection.

As for the other woman, I met her a few months later. She and I were both on a board of directors for a nonprofit ministry. She was the board president. We got to know each other through that interaction, and I felt the same gut response: this woman is meant to be my friend.

Now the three of us are really bonded and lean on one another for support.

How can you get to a great place of having other women in your life who understand your business journey *and* the challenge of blending it with your personal life? One, you have to get out there. You're not going to meet anybody if you don't leave your house or office! Two, you also need to listen to that little bit of intuition. You know when you sense you need to know a person? You're not sure why, but you have the feeling you two can connect? That's when you should most definitely be brave and take that step to reach out and ask them for a cup of coffee or lunch. Have that deeper conversation.

It could be a person you meet in the grocery store or someone who lives in the same building. It could be an attendee at a business event you show up at and have never met before. But you have to follow those gut instincts. Our intuition usually leads us pretty clearly in the right direction. And when we follow those nudges to see where they go, it can have a significant impact on our lives. So I encourage you to be open to making those friendships and then have some really authentic conversations. You'll be glad you did.

#

I also want to touch on the needs of working women with children. I've already addressed this topic, but *I found that I could never hear words of support enough when I was working with kids at home.*

So here I go again! This is for you working moms who don't quite know how you're going to keep on keeping on. You may be thinking you don't have any more knots to tie onto the end of your rope. You're wondering when you're going to be able to sit down for ten minutes without your phone pinging or a child asking for something. You wonder if and when you will ever get to Hawaii, or whatever the vacay of your dreams is. And are your days of jumping on top of a bar to sing a karaoke song over for good? Remember that lighthearted person? Where is she? You're afraid you'll never be that woman again. The thought makes you cry so hard in the shower, you stay in until the water runs cold.

I've been there. I swear.

I think the biggest thing is that you just have to give yourself some grace. It's OK to want to be successful in your career and be a great mom, and you can do both of those things. But perfection isn't attainable. It's not! And don't forget that full-time, stay-at-home moms or full-time career women with no kids can't achieve perfection, either.

We are all human. Humans mess up. Humans who are perfect *don't exist*. And who would want to be friends with a perfect human, anyway? Ugh!

As women we have to give one another support and acknowledgment that we don't have to be perfect. We don't have to follow the textbook of what moms are supposed to be like. Other moms' experiences are theirs, not yours. You have to figure out what works for you. What do you want to teach your kids? How do you want them to grow up?

Above all, give yourself some *grace*. Progress and momentum are good. But they are sometimes messy, other times ugly, and often painful. Yet at the end of the day, you're still taking steps forward. Sure, there might be a step back, or a zigzag, but *take the long view*. Please do that. Take. The. Long. View. That advice deserves emphasis after every word. Taking the long view has saved my mental health so many times. On those days that I feel like a failure, if I pull back the camera, look up, and see the timeline of my life with my kids, I see we have made huge progress! In fact, I go from being down in the dumps to feeling like Rocky after he won that boxing match against all the odds.

In the long run, our children are resilient, and they're going to be OK if we're not the ones who drop them off at school, pick them up from school, and help them do their homework. Quality time is what matters most. Believe that. Ignore the folks who say quantity time is everything. Sure, quantity time is nice. Life is short. And the years we have with our children will fly by. That being said, *it's far more important for us to be truly present with our kids in the time we have with them than to be distracted.*

So however many minutes of the day you can give your children, be there 100 percent. They will notice and appreciate that far more than if you're there in name only. Kids can sense when parents have other things on their minds.

This is something I tell my kids over and over: "I know I'm not perfect, but I love you, and I'm doing the very best I can with the information I have." That works for them. They understand that I'm learning, I'm evolving, and hopefully getting better, just like they are. They are aware that not every decision I make will be the right one and not every action will be the best one. But they know I'll do the best I can with what I have.

That's enough. I'm enough. And my kids are getting the message, through my example, that *they* are enough. That's probably the biggest takeaway I want them to have from their childhood. It's such a simple goal—to want our kids to believe they are enough—but bringing up children can sometimes be a complicated business, whether you work or not, in spite of how simple the precepts of good parenting are (to love those little suckers with all your heart and keep them alive until they're adults and responsible for themselves).

Let's stick with simplifying our lives as working mothers as best we can. I have many irons in the fire at all times, so when it comes to my children, I stay aligned with my values as a parent by focusing on two big things: stability and visibility.

While they're learning, growing, and doing things on their own, I want to keep the family ship *stable* and be in their sights, or *visible*—maybe off to the right, on the horizon, or up close, depending on where they need me to be.

Stability and visibility. Everything else can go out the window. Truly. Toss it all. As long as you have those two things, your kids have what they need to do well. When your homelife is stable, and you're not far away if they need your help, you're probably going to raise independent, curious children. And that's a good portent for them becoming productive, happy adults. When children know that their parent has their back, they give themselves permission to be brave, to explore their passions, to not be stymied by failure.

My kids are very healthy and independent. That's by the grace of God and good genes from their grandparents and great-grandparents, but I'd like to say it's also because of my adherence to the principles of stability and visibility. I was there overseeing, but I didn't do everything for them. We had a home structure that was clear to them because I made sure I communicated expectations. They had to help around the house. They had to earn their allowance. They had to pay their own gas money for their cars. They had to do the dishes every day, and they had chores every week. Things weren't just handed to them. They had to earn rewards, and when they did, I reminded them that they'd worked for those rewards. I also encouraged them to try new things for the sheer pleasure of exploring life and all it has to offer. We talked about the things that excited them. And I listened. A lot.

Don't get me wrong. Plenty of times, I wasn't physically present while our relationship as parent and child evolved. I was at work or volunteering or making dinner. But I was involved very much in their lives. They couldn't sideskirt me. I was the immovable rock, much to their dismay sometimes, as teenagers. They knew the targets they had to reach and that there would be ongoing discussions, on the phone and in person, about their progress. And yes, about their passions, about the people they were becoming.

Stability and visibility. It was one of my favorite mantras. I clung to it through every professional and personal storm. And how did my approach pay off?

As I said earlier (and it's worth repeating because all working mothers need to hear it's possible for them, too), my kids are productive and happy. And much to my delight, all three have some sort of entrepreneurial activity going on right now. It's so much fun to see!

My oldest daughter is a professional photographer. She started it as a little side hustle when she was in college, and it's now her full-time career. It gives her the flexibility to be home with her kids and to set her own schedule but still work and contribute and follow her own passions. She's very successful at it and has won some national and international recognition. One way she gives back—because her daughter and my granddaughter Iris was a NICU baby—is to do photo sessions in the NICU with the babies and their families.

My youngest daughter runs a thrift store online. She buys or picks up clothing, upcycles it—which is so cool and creative of her— and then sells it. Sustainability is her passion, and she's making money by following the desire of her heart.

My son is just starting off. In fact, a short while ago I helped him get his Employer Identification Number and register with the state of South Dakota. So, he's going to officially start his business refinishing and repairing pool tables. Someone's got to do that! I'm proud of him and his two sisters for working in fields that truly interest them. They know how important it is to love their work—because then it doesn't feel like work.

It's especially heartening for me to see my kids become interested in creating their own businesses because I'm really a first-generation entrepreneur. My dad took a stab at working independently as an electrician, but most of the time, he worked for other people. It just wasn't in my family's mindset, and that's OK. It's good when each generation that comes along finds more opportunity. For my kids, it's natural for them to think about being bosses of their own companies, and I know my parents and grandparents would love that develop-ment in the family outlook. It's the American dream.

And hey, back to being perfect and how impossible that is, and how it's not really helpful. I'm not saying I was or am perfect when it comes to helping my kids develop an entrepreneurial mindset. I could have done a better job sharing the challenges that come with it. At one point, it became clear to me that they thought Mom making money running her own company was easy and that there wasn't a lot of sacrifice or commitment.

Which of course is not the case. So I have had to be more intentional about sharing the struggles and the challenges, even as my children age up and gift me with grandkids. I've begun to lean harder into having them help me process issues I've had blending work and homelife. I might say, "OK, guys, this is a really stressful week for me, and there's a lot going on. This is what's happening, X and Y and Z. I need you to give me a little bit of grace if it takes me longer to call you back, or if I can't help you this week with babysitting." Or whatever the current family needs are.

But I remind them that the end goal is that I will have more freedom and flexibility to be able to babysit more often in the future if I can get through this week's challenge at work. So I try to help them understand more. I didn't at first. And as a result, they thought it was a pretty seamless process: you decide you're going to start a company, you do it and it all works, money flows in, and life is good.

Haha!

I've been much more intentional lately about sharing some of the challenges. The great thing is that being so mature now, they not only get it better, but they also appreciate what I've accomplished way more than they did when they were younger.

In conclusion, I'd like to share my top five points for working women who have big dreams and maybe not enough support to get there:

The first thing I'd recommend is to *find a coach*. Find somebody you can trust, with whom you can speak openly about your challenges and frustrations. You can't really talk to your employees about employee situations, and financial issues, and the struggles of managing. This is why it's so important to find a coach you really believe in and trust. It's probably going to be somebody you pay. But whoever it is, they need to be willing to be your sounding board. It helps if they can be reasonable when you're making emotional decisions. We all have to make those tough calls. A reasonable coach might come in and say, "Do you think maybe that's a bit of an emotional decision, and have you thought about it this other way?"

At the very least, your coach should be someone who can help you learn and grow, as well as challenge you to be better.

The second point I'd suggest is to *find that inner circle of friends* who can provide emotional support to back up the guidance, encouragement, and sometimes pushback that you get from a business coach. These are people who will give you unconditional support. It was so helpful for me to be able to trust and especially to be completely raw with other women. Whoever comprises your circle, you're utterly transparent and connect at the soul level. You should be able to say to them, "I just need to cry today. So can I come over to your house and cry for a little bit? And then we'll have a cup of coffee, and it'll be fine. But I just need to cry for a little bit," and not feel judged because you're needing to do that.

The third thing is to *take time for your own health and wellness* because we take on a lot. Usually, we take on way more than we should. That's what we do as women. We want to care for everybody, and we want everything to be perfect for everybody else. But we need to remember our own selves. Having a routine, or a practice, or an exercise for self-help or self-care is so important. I go to the gym at least four days a week, and it's a great stress reliever. Some days it's difficult to get it scheduled in, but I feel better when I do it.

I also schedule a ninety-minute massage every month as part of my wellness. I'd rather do that than pay for a mani-pedi. I do my own nails so that I have money to do the massage. But do whatever works for you.

Take vacations. That's definitely part of wellness. Take a vacation where you really fully disconnect. I would recommend that you do this at least one week each time, twice a year. It takes at least seven days for you to leave work, wind down, and have a few days of relaxation before you start winding back up to go back to your regular life. And don't forget that your business will be fine. In fact, the business will be stronger because you do it, whether you are the only employee or you have a team of people you can leave it to.

Number four is to *have a set structure or routine* that's not only predictable for you but also predictable for your family. I actually learned this from my son, who has ADHD.

If we didn't have a very structured routine and he didn't know exactly what to expect every day, day in and day out, it would be absolute chaos.

I've learned also from my team at work that if they don't know what's expected of them every day—what time they're supposed to show up, what work they're supposed to do, and when they can take breaks—they fall apart, too. Routines lower people's stress levels so they can think about what they need to think about.

As for yourself, having routines ensures you'll get your self-care each day. But also, routines allow you to turn off at the end of the night. We really need to be able to disconnect and take that brain break at the end of the day, to go home and be present for our families. If our schedules are too fluid, or not really clearly defined, it's really hard to make the shift both physically and mentally between work and our personal lives. Suddenly, one takes over, and you don't have time for anything else.

I'm not going to lie. For me, the routine for a long time was working six days a week. That's what I had to do when I first started. But I would always take one day off. I was very, very disciplined that I would not work one day a week. And it wasn't always a Sunday or a Saturday. It wasn't always the same day. But I would make sure I had at least one full day every week that I didn't work.

Having some structure around your day—some definition around the time and space—is better for you. You're setting a good example for the people you lead, and it's better for your family because they know what to expect. Overall, routine boosts your mental health.

The fifth suggestion I have is to *engage in groups*. Be a part of a network or community. It can be a group inside or outside your industry. But surround yourself with people who will challenge you and are also invested in helping you. It could be a professional group, church group, or a neighborhood watch party group. I don't think it matters what the group is, as long as it's fulfilling something in you and pushing you to be better. Hopefully, it's teaching you better com-munication skills and helping you develop your leadership skills. It's always a bonus if there are opportunities to serve on different boards, groups, or committees.

It could also be an outlet for one of your passions. We have one employee who is in very much a technical role but has a strong creative interest in painting. He's in a group that allows him to indulge that love. Anything that brings you joy enhances your life at home and at work—and those of the people who surround you.

This group is keeping you connected and keeping you grounded. You're giving back and also growing yourself. It's a mutual thing.

# "You Betcha"s

1. You betcha we need more women CEOs, managers, and entrepreneurs!

2. You betcha we get a lot farther working together than we do staying in our own lane.

3. You betcha all women deserve to put their needs and wants at the top of their list of priorities.

# Creating Your Legacy

*No one is useless in this world who*
*lightens the burdens of another.*
**—CHARLES DICKENS**

You probably don't wake up every day thinking, "Today I'm building my legacy." But each day, we're doing just that. Someday we'll be known only by what we leave behind. And why is that important? Our legacy illuminates our priorities in life, usually. It's what we focus on enough to leave a mark. So in a way, our legacies reveal who we choose to be.

A legacy is meant to be a gift you leave the world without expecting an ROI. It can be a physical offering to someone you care about, or an institution you admire, such as money in a bank account or a house or a property. And while recipients of those gifts may find them meaningful, an intangible legacy may resonate even more. Not all of us will be in a position to leave wealth to our loved ones. What cherished beliefs, values, or traditions can you pass down to your children, friends, family, and community to embrace after you're gone? Those principles and habits are your legacy, too, and they are within everyone's reach.

People with hearts and healthy mindsets don't want to leave behind a negative legacy. Yet some people manage to, willingly or not. The last thing most of us want is for the people we leave behind to jettison memories of us. But it happens. In Charles Dickens's story of the bitter skinflint Scrooge, the main character gets a second chance to change his tarnished legacy, which accrued slowly over the years as he rejected opportunities to show loving kindness to other people. Scrooge was lucky. In real life, none of us will get a do-over. It's a good reminder that how we act on a daily basis is probably more our legacy than anything else.

Not many people actually think about legacy building, but we should because we all leave one, whether we think about it or not. What's important to you? What brings your life meaning? What are you about? Can you distill your life's purpose into a sentence? It's worth a try. Once you realize who you are and what you stand for, how can you move in a focused direction to create a lasting footprint that celebrates you and your purpose long after you're gone?

I know. It's a lot. And we only have so much time left to figure this out and get cracking. But instead of being intimidated, look up with me. Take a breath. We were not meant to constantly live in the future and focus on the end of our lives. We are meant to mostly stay here, in the present, being grateful for what we have at the current moment. Really, a legacy is only our doing the best we can on ordinary days to make a difference for the better. That's not so intimidating to think about, is it? Those routine days add up, and before you know it, you've established your legacy without even realizing it.

But if legacy building as a very intentional, long-term activity excites you, by all means, get going shaping yours formally, on paper, and with attorneys if you're gifting property (you can do this in a will, but sometimes special endowments require extra steps). I enjoy planning and developing my legacy. I want to leave some wealth for my kids and grandkids but not so much that they lose interest in finding their own purpose. I'd like to think that my personal values will be passed down and appreciated by them, too. I'm also interested in endowing some nonprofits I admire with financial gifts that will help keep them thriving.

## THOUGHTSHOT

Overall, I tend to think that my day-to-day choices are where most of my legacy lies. It's in the little things, you know? Getting an employee a cup of coffee with two creamers and one sugar, just how they like it. Picking up the phone to advise my child on a matter of the heart. Petting an adorable dog that walks by my office and chatting with the shy, elderly stranger who owns it. That's the Korena I hope everyone will remember.

*Who is the you that you'd like everyone to remember? Are you close to being that person? Are you that person already? How can you enhance your legacy even more?*

In case you're wondering, there's no one way to build a legacy. There's so much personal accountability around the idea because it's you! It's the choices *you* make in life, the dreams *you* have, the goals *you* set. You have to be willing to do the work. And don't settle for what other people tell you to do or not to do. I can't tell you how many times somebody told me that I couldn't do something or that I wouldn't be successful. When I was first pregnant, I heard, "You can't keep this baby because you're too young." And then it was, "You can't go to college because you have a child." Followed by, "You're never going to be successful in this career because you're _____." Fill in the blank with any number of negative words.

Throughout my entire career, there were always naysayers. And there will always be people who tell you that you can't or you shouldn't. You simply have to believe in yourself enough to take the risk and try whatever it is you want to do. Because if you don't try it, you're never going to know.

And I swear it's OK if it doesn't work the way you thought it was going to work the first time. That doesn't mean it's a failure. And that doesn't mean you won't have an opportunity to edit it, tweak or change it, and try again. Because you don't really know what the right fit is, or what that right thing is for you, until you step into it and give it a shot.

Thomas Edison tried two thousand materials before he found the right filament for the light bulb. If he'd have given up on the first try, or been afraid to even attempt it the first time, where would we be today? Crediting the invention of the light bulb to someone else, that's where! (Surely, it would have been invented eventually.)

> So you've tried things and failed, as we all do. But have you tried two thousand times?
>
> Name something you've failed at that you will consider trying again, in light of Edison's unflagging efforts to make that light bulb shine.

Do you really want someone else braver than you to get credit for doing the things you wish you'd had the guts to try?

When we watch Olympic athletes, we're seeing them in their prime. They're at the top of their sport, the best of the best. We witness three days of glory they've achieved. What we don't see is the twenty years of six-hours-a-day, seven-days-a-week training that got them to that point.

We need to believe in ourselves enough to push forward and to do the things we want to do. There are going to be bumps and bruises. I can almost guarantee it's never going to work perfectly. You'll fall and pick yourself up a lot. But that's OK. Life is messy. And so what if it is? Most people aren't going to see the messy except you, anyway. So much of creating our lives is about accepting that we are imperfect and trying anyway, over and over, if we have to.

As you think about your own legacy and what brings meaning to your life, you might be wondering what brings meaning to mine. I'm happy to share. I've told you how important it is for me to nurture other people in both my personal and professional life. I want people to feel seen and appreciated. It's who I am, in a nutshell. So for me, success isn't about money. I've never really cared that much about it. Yes, I like to be able to take my kids on vacations, and I love being able to pay my bills without being stressed about it.

But meaning for me has never come from building massive amounts of wealth. I find meaning at work by building a better organization that shows my employees that it's possible to have a successful career and still keep their family priorities first.

Meaning for me also comes from exposing my clients to cool technology that's available at the enterprise level of organizations like Coca-Cola and NPR. I want to bring that level of sophistication down to the mainstream and make it accessible to everybody. I don't want any business owner to be told that they can't do something because they don't have a sufficient budget. If they want to be successful, if they want to grow their business, and if they're willing to jump in and experiment a little bit with technology, they can take on the big players on a level playing field, using the technology that we have available today.

For me, that is where I find my purpose as an entrepreneur: seeing other people be successful, whether they are companies we work with or my own employees. I feel fulfilled when I can use my skills and influence to make life better for somebody else.

Again, that goes for my personal life, too. I want to help. I want to be there. I want to celebrate other people's victories and lend a helping hand when they're down. I may be a tough cookie when I have to be. But above all, I'm about the warm-and-fuzzies: hope, love, and celebrating being alive.

I take baby steps every day toward building my legacy by choosing to be of service every way I can at home and at work. But I also use honest-to-goodness planning techniques to achieve my business aims. I'm a big Hashtag Goals person, don't forget. One of the processes we use at KeyMedia is called Traction EOS. We start by setting a ten-year vision. We cast what we want that ten-year vision to look like, and then we break it down into parts.

We ask ourselves, what goals can we set for the next three years to get us closer to that ten-year vision? And then we break that down: what do we have to do this year to be there in three years? And we step it back even further by establishing our one-year objectives, things we have to check off this year to be a year closer to our three-year mark.

Then from there, we break it down into quarterly chunks, or rocks. That is, to hit those year-end objectives, what do we have to do this quarter? And then we break those objectives down into milestones over that ninety-day window.

It's a great system that we follow religiously at KeyMedia. All of us use a web-based program to keep track, and we do weekly meetings to check in on our progress. Sometimes we meet multiple times per week. We also do quarterly meetings where we review where we're at and what's next.

It works really well. Making a concentrated effort to stay aligned with my vision for the future of my company means I'm also staying on track building my legacy. It's a two-for-one deal!

At KeyMedia, we love seeing our goal-setting pay off. We're in a rapidly changing environment and industry, so that means every day we face a lot of exciting challenges. Working in digital media and technology, we see that the technology is evolving faster than we can keep up with most of the time, even though we have a fairly large team dedicated to monitoring those changes.

A lot of privacy regulation is coming through, too, which complicates things. And another challenge is transitioning from Baby Boomers to Millennials to Gen X-ers taking over as advancements in artificial intelligence (AI) and machine learning come down the pike and the demographics of the workforce evolve.

For us, what will have the greatest impact on our ability to do outstanding work is becoming experts not just in technology but also in data management. We want to help our clients understand the information they currently have available to them that they've collected over the years of running their businesses.

Our job is to identify where that data lives and figure out how to break it down and put it together so that we can draw individual insights and find client journeys and trends specific to their customers, based on their experiences. And then we will build that out and use that information moving forward to do personalized marketing as well as automated marketing and streamline it.

This means we can evaluate the information faster, and we get smarter decisions made in a shorter window of time. But we're also applying those results in real time versus waiting until a year-end evaluation, or until something's not working the way it's supposed to.

This year we're launching a whole data sciences service to help customers accomplish those goals. It's taken us about three years of research and development because we're not finding anybody else who has an established process for it. There are companies that do parts of it but nobody who really can help from start to finish. It's been a long learning curve, and obviously, as we're learning, the technology changes! So we have to relearn, adapt, and evolve as it's happening.

But it's thrilling to see it all come to fruition. When you've been working on something for so long and people don't understand what you're doing or why you're doing it, you have to stay true to your vision and keep pushing forward on it.

Right now, we're soft-introducing our efforts to a few people, and they're very excited about it. We're getting great feedback. And because everything looks so promising, KeyMedia is investing in a space that's triple the size of our current one. While most people are abandoning office space, we're doubling down and going all in to create an environment that provides us opportunity for growth.

That's so me. It goes back to being willing to step outside and do something that others aren't willing to do. In 2018, a group wanted to create an event around marketing AI because it was evolving. But people weren't understanding it. So we all got together to talk about marketing AI, what was happening, how it was happening, what we did know, and what we didn't know. At that point, there was a lot more that we didn't know.

But for me, a light bulb went off, and I thought, "Oh my gosh, this is going to change everything we're doing." And so I really became a student and started to study marketing AI to figure out what it did mean for us at KeyMedia—not only how it would change what we were doing but also how it could *improve* what we were doing.

At this point of AI marketing technology's evolution, customers don't need to be experts in it, but they do need somebody like KeyMedia to help them figure out how to take what information they have and make it actionable.

I'm proud that we've been ahead of the curve and invested so much time and energy and resources into becoming marketing AI experts. We've got a full-time researcher joining our team and a year's worth of key insights we took away from our research that we're going to be distributing throughout the year. We're meeting with and introducing a couple of key clients soon, and because marketing AI is still relatively new and unproven, my intention is to onboard one client about every two months for the first year and really perfect it. And then we'll open the floodgates. We want to be a marketing technology company, and we want to help our customers better use the technology that's available to them to get better outcomes.

So I have these big goals. I'm going to share them with you because yes, it's cool to see what other people are doing, right? It's inspiring. It's educational. But I have another reason I'm sharing the deets with you that I'll talk about afterward.

In the next five years, there's a lot going on. I think my staff will double. And I've told you about our new space, which is four times the size of the previous space. The property side of the business is where I want to build a long-term legacy for my kids, driving recurring revenue for them. They're not at all interested in the advertising side.

Within the next five years, I need to have my exit strategy down: focusing on who I'm transitioning the advertising business to and what that's going to look like. By year seven, I anticipate being on a board of directors and guiding the person running the advertising side of the business. So I've got a couple of years to train them. And then I see myself stepping back and letting them take over and start making decisions. By year ten, I'm pretty much out, and they're running the show.

I don't think our company will ever grow to its full potential only working out of Sioux Falls, so we'll have offices in multiple locations. We've had full-time remote employees since before COVID-19, and it has always worked well for us. We're a technology company; if we can't figure out how to conduct business from anywhere, then I don't know who can. In fact, I would love to open an office in Florida and be there all winter long—not spend my winters in South Dakota.

So that's the plan. But to get there, I have to trust a lot of other people.

This is where all those details I shared with you about my plans intersect with a crucial point I was saving back: *I need to rely on other people to help me make all my big plans happen.* Another way to put it is: *I can't reach my goals on my own.*

It seems so obvious. But it's probably the biggest challenge for most entrepreneurs, all of whom think they're pretty brilliant. Otherwise, they wouldn't start a company. For some reason, learning to let go and trust their teams is the hardest thing for a good entrepreneur to learn. But if you forget to do that, the proverbial you-know-what will hit the fan. You'll struggle. No one will be happy. And those goals? You might as well kiss them goodbye.

So to those of you who employ people, I have this to say: I sure hope you're managing them well. Otherwise, you might as well go home and give up.

I feel very strongly about this. It all goes back to treating people the way you'd like to be treated. When you value your employees, you mentor them and allow them to make mistakes as they grow, the same way you'd give your children the grace to mature.

I invest in my people and empower them so they're not reliant specifically on me to make every decision about how to handle every event and to do their jobs well. Our clients need to have relationships with people outside of their connection to me. Our team needs to be empowered to feel like they can handle the things that come up and that I'm not a bottleneck. Things need to be able to happen without my involvement in them. It's all about training, investing, and encouraging them to step into leadership roles. I want them to take an active role in what's happening and where things are going. But I need to allow them the space to do it.

*Above all, they're not going to do it exactly the way I would do it, and I have to be OK with that.* I have to accept the fact that they've got other ideas that are probably pretty good—and I don't have all the answers. I can share my experiences, and I can walk alongside them, and I can share how I would do things. But the best thing I can do is ask the team to explain to me why they did something a certain way, how they came to that conclusion. I ask them to talk me through their thought process. If I can understand the way they're thinking about it, I can understand how they got to the end and help them either get there more efficiently, faster, or just let them go and do it their way because it doesn't need to change.

You have to be willing to trust. It's scary to give people space. But I found in my experience, when I trust people, or tell them, or show them that I trust them, they rise to the occasion 99 percent of the time. It's one of those things that was explained to me by one of the coaches I had recently. In most organizations, no employee has the autonomy to write a check for $100,000 and not be questioned. However, everybody in an organization has the ability to make an error that would cost the company $100,000.

That's daunting. So how do we equip our employees with the knowledge, the confidence, and the expertise to avoid those errors?

Even with the best training, big errors happen. And in our industry, we're moving incredibly fast, working with technology that's often unproven. Things go wrong outside of our control and sometimes within our control. My first question when there's a problem is always, "What happened? What did you learn from it? And what are you going to do differently?"

If we don't have an organization where people are empowered to make mistakes or to try something new, or to push the boundaries a little bit, we're going to become extinct. We must create that environment where it's OK to experiment, to step into something that's different. And it's OK if it doesn't work the way we think it's going to work.

When we're transparent, when we communicate and talk about what's happening, about what we expect to happen, and about what really happens, most of the time it all works out. But we still need to take on that mantle of risk. It's part of the industry I'm in.

Over the years, I've come to believe that most legacy building happens around the concept of service. I try to live a "Do unto others" kind of life. We all have a talent we can offer somewhere, a way that we can contribute. But have you ever noticed you can't give what you don't have? I sure have. Plenty of times I've wanted to go the extra mile to help someone or contribute to a cause, but I've run out of steam or money.

It's true: Whatever resources keep us functioning in this world, they'll eventually run out. We have to keep replenishing them, whether it's physical energy, emotional stamina, knowledge of a certain subject, or our bank accounts.

New growth has to happen for us to keep going forward. It's a law of nature. Growth equals longevity equals survival.

This is why one of the core values of my company is growth. I want to create a place that provides personal and professional development opportunities every single day so that when people leave the company—I never pretend they'll be with me their whole careers!—they leave better than when they started. I'm happy if they're able to find a job more aligned with what they need to reach their dreams. I'm proud that KeyMedia was able to help them identify and build out those big goals when they were with me.

Growth happens with community service, too. We have an innate responsibility to leave this world better than it was when we started. For some people, that's volunteering; for others, it's creative work or legal work, or whatever brings them joy. One should always be joyful when giving, by the way. Choose something that makes you happy.

I attribute a lot of my career success to my willingness to give, share, and collaborate. That giving helps me grow. And it created a community of people around me that supported me back.

I especially think we should get involved with any opportunity that aligns with the skills we have. For me, that led me to a professor in college who introduced me to the world of media; he helped me get my first job at a TV station that I worked at on weekends while I was still in school. That position opened the door into a world I didn't even know existed when I started college. And then a mentor at my first agency taught me everything I needed to know on media planning, negotiating, and strategy. I was about as green as you can get, but she spent five years pouring everything she knew into me. To this day, I still have a very high regard for her because she was so fundamental in formulating my passion for the industry. There's no way I would ever be where I am today without her.

So now I've come to a point in my career where I get to be that person and help others get started building their careers and figuring out what they love and are passionate about. I get to help establish the framework for their future success.

Every time we look up from our fixed perspective to share our time, treasure, and talent with other people, we're striving upward. We're growing. We're new. That's what life is—one long journey of becoming until we draw our last breath. Growth is the key to living a fulfilling life. So to celebrate this amazing fact, and our truly precious existence, I came up with a breakdown of the word *growth* and what that idea means to me in light of what I've learned over my long career. I'm sharing it with you, my family, friends, colleagues, and my employees in the hopes you'll draw some inspiration from it.

The letter *g* in *growth* represents *giving*. Every living thing has to surrender part of itself in order to thrive or grow. A pine tree releases a seed. A person exhales a breath. It's in the giving that we transcend who we were and become who we are now and who we are meant to be in the future. Share your time and talent.

The letter *r* stands for *receiving*. You have to be willing to take what's being offered. You have to be humble enough to say yes, I want to learn, and I *can* learn from you. I'm willing to receive what you're teaching me. Receive coaching and feedback.

The letter *o* in the word *growth* stands for *opportunity*. You have to be open to seeking out and recognizing opportunities. Then you need to take advantage of the opportunity when it's there.

I tell my team members that if they want to attend any training, or if they want to do any personal development, if they want to do any online or in-person courses, they just literally have to fill out a form and we'll pay for it.

The letter *w* stands for *weighing*. Part of growth is weighing, or evaluating, your progress. What's the point of working toward something if you're confused about where you stand and you don't even see your target?

In orienteering, which is the practice of finding your way using a compass and a map, the traveler will stop now and then to check their compass heading. Being off even a half of a degree can eventually land that person far, far away from their intended destination. It's crucial to maintain accuracy with the compass readings.

Stopping, weighing your situation, and regrouping are essential parts of growth.

The *t* in *growth* stands for *tackling*. You have to tackle the uncomfortable to truly grow. You have to get outside your comfort zone, not shy away from the hard stuff.

The *h* stands for *honor*. You want to honor those who have come before you by carrying their wisdom forward, along with your own. And you want to also honor those who come after you by creating opportunities for them to be and do better. Ultimately, that's what growth is about: reaching our potential. And we always want the next generation to exceed ours.

My story may resonate with you in its entirety or in small pieces. It's not always been an easy route, but it has been entirely mine—mistakes and celebrations, joy and pain. Each of these events has provided me with the wisdom, strength, and motivation to get up and go another day. Each experience teaches me a lesson that allows me to grow, personally or professionally.

The intention when I started the journey of this book was not to bolster my own confidence (or bore you with my Midwest upbringing) but to encourage those that have struggled or are struggling. To show you are not alone, that your past does not define your future. Own your story, the highs and lows and everything in between, because yours might be the next bestseller.

## "You Betcha"s

1. You betcha everyone leaves a legacy, whether they mean to or not. So it's best to consider what you want your footprint to be.

2. You betcha working on a ten-year plan for your company will help you stay focused on your big goals, and it will double as legacy planning.

3. You betcha entrepreneurs with employees will fail if they don't build trust with their team.

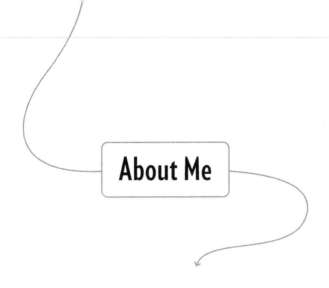

# About Me

Looking back over my fifty-some years on this earth, I am confident in stating I have a good life! I am grateful for every struggle and appreciate each accomplishment. But starting out in life was challenging, and my path is not that of a traditional business owner. In my life, there have been defining moments, moments I can still see clearly today, which have changed the trajectory of my life.

Delivering my first child at age seventeen cemented my first commitment to my children—they would not have a life of poverty or be dependent on welfare. Because of this, I worked three jobs and attended college full time while being a single mom.

Years later, when my middle child was fourteen, came the second commitment. On that day, my son stated he felt my job was more important than his game. To him, this was a passing comment without any weight. To me, it was a crushing blow that resulted in me leaving a company I loved and stepping blindly into entrepreneurship.

There are more that you will identify as you read the chapters of my life. They have given me the motivation to persevere. My *why* when people ask how or why I do what I do. It has led me to where I stand today, the visionary and CEO of two thriving businesses, a mom and grandma, a wife, and a mentor. This is the clarity that founded the values and vision for my company—to prove it is possible to have a successful career that supports your family without sacrificing your time and life for that same family. It drives all decisions on benefits, company perks, on who is hired and who is released.

My *why* has also given me the desire to be the best, to break ceilings, and bust molds. I started a programmatic digital marketing agency in small-town Colton, South Dakota, when most people didn't even know how to advertise on Google. I was the fifty-sixth professional in the nation to achieve the Internet Advertising Bureau's Digital Media Sales Certification—a brand-new program to test one's application of knowledge and ethical standards in an industry resembling the Wild West. My company has been recognized nationally for excellence, innovation, and delivering results.

Along the journey, I came to realize the anomaly of it all. Less than 4 percent of women-owned small businesses (WOSBs) ever break $1 million in revenue (KeyMedia accomplished this in two years). Most WOSBs never have more than two employees or make it past three years (KeyMedia is currently at fourteen employees and thirteen years). To do this from where I started—a teen mom needing welfare to feed my child—only stacks the deck further against me. But I am confident in saying that if I can do it, so can you.

# Get In Touch

If my story resonated with you, I would be honored to connect, hear your story, or go deeper into mine.

*www.facebook.com/korena.keys*
*www.linkedin.com/in/korena*

---

KeyMedia Solutions is a digital media firm working with advertising agencies and internal marketing teams. Our mission is to provide access to world-class technology, build cross-media integrations, and analyze data to deliver measurable results through marketing/advertising dollars. Connect through our website or social media pages.

*www.KeyMedia.solutions*
*www.facebook.com/KeyMediaSolutions*
*www.linkedin.com/company/key-media-solutions*

---

If you are looking for a speaker for an upcoming event, you will find more information at *www.korenakeys.com.*

Printed in the USA
CPSIA information can be obtained
at www.ICGtesting.com
JSHW021947200524
63489JS00005B/379